Black Loyalists in New Brunswick

Black Loyalists in New Brunswick

STEPHEN DAVIDSON

FORMAC PUBLISHING COMPANY LIMITED
HALIFAX

Formac Publishing Company Limited recognizes the support of the Province of Nova Scotia through Film and Creative Industries Nova Scotia. We are pleased to work in partnership with the Province of Nova Scotia to develop and promote our creative industries for the benefit of all Nova Scotians. We acknowledge the support of the Canada Council for the Arts which last year invested $157 million to bring the arts to Canadians throughout the country.

Canada NOVA SCOTIA Canada Council for the Arts Conseil des Arts du Canada

Cover design: Tyler Cleroux
Cover image: Joseph Brown Comingo, painting: *View of Saint John, New Brunswick, 1814*, The New Brunswick Museum, (1966.100A)

Painted thirty-one years after the Loyalist evacuation to Saint John in 1783, Comingo's watercolour is a glimpse of New Brunswick's largest city as many of the Black Loyalists in this book would have known it. The absence of Black people in Comingo's depiction reflects the time and place: under Saint John's 1785 charter, Blacks were prohibited from living or working in the city unless granted special license by the mayor. The exclusion is also emblematic of this era, from which no contemporary images of New Brunswick's Black Loyalists have been discovered. In the centre foreground, Comingo situates three formally dressed Indigenous figures (likely Mi'kmaq or Wolastoqiyik) as the painting's focal point. The figures in red (centre, background) would be British soldiers from the garrison at Fort Howe (far left, background), while the two women (left, foreground) convey that a sense of elegant leisure is enjoyed by some in the colony.

Library and Archives Canada Cataloguing in Publication

Title: Black loyalists in New Brunswick : the lives of eight African Americans in colonial New Brunswick 1783-1834 / Stephen Davidson.
Names: Davidson, Stephen Eric, 1953- author.
Description: Includes bibliographical references and index.
Identifiers: Canadiana (print) 20200162136 | Canadiana (ebook) 20200162144 | ISBN 9781459506169 (softcover) | ISBN 9781459506176 (EPUB)
Subjects: LCSH: African American loyalists—New Brunswick—Biography. | CSH: Black loyalists—New Brunswick—Biography. | LCGFT: Biographies.
Classification: LCC FC2500.B6 D38 2020 | DDC 971.5/100496073—dc23

Formac Publishing Company Limited
5502 Atlantic Street
Halifax, Nova Scotia, Canada
B3H 1G4
www.formac.ca

Printed and bound in Canada.

Contents

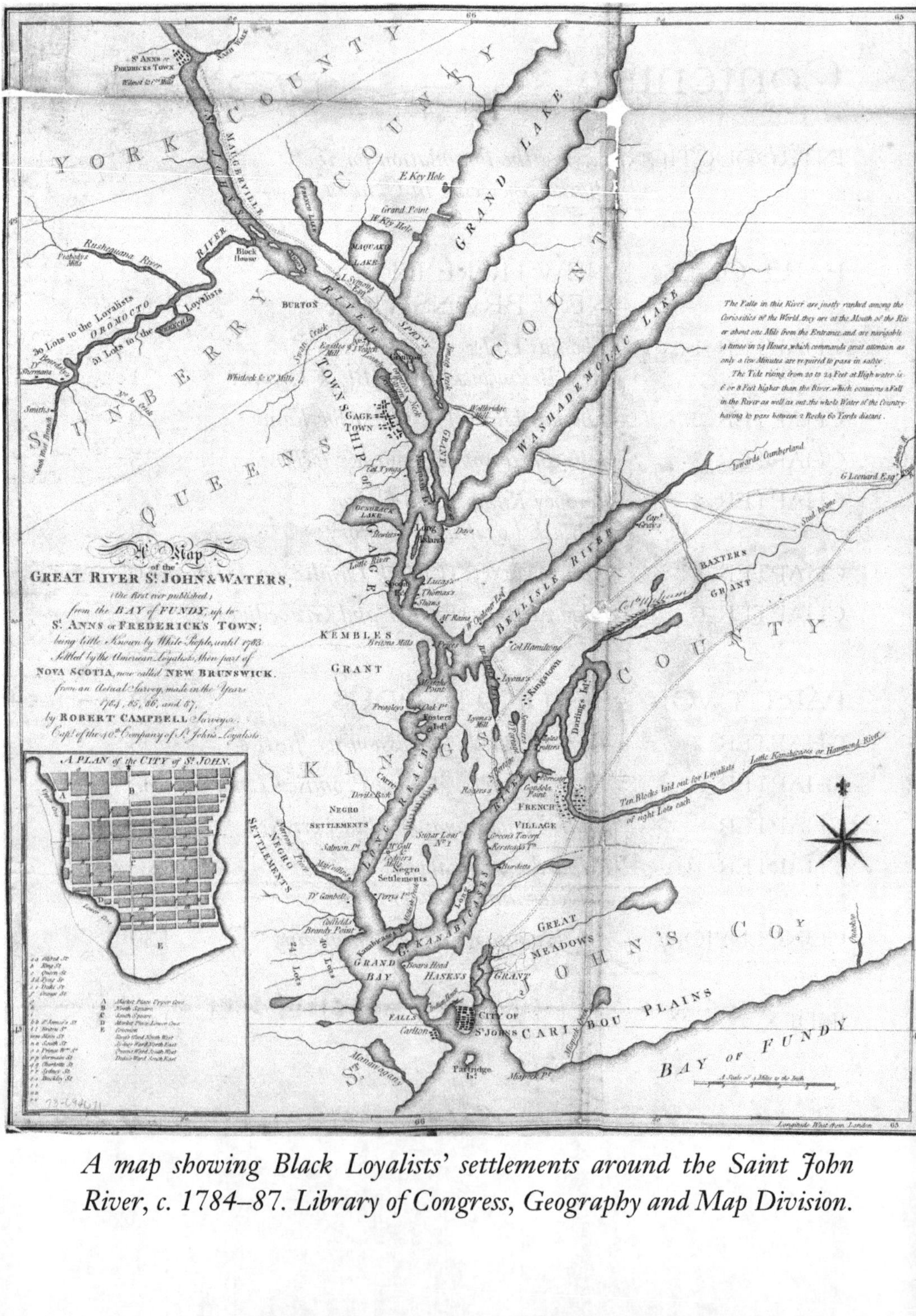

A map showing Black Loyalists' settlements around the Saint John River, c. 1784–87. Library of Congress, Geography and Map Division.

INTRODUCTION

Laying the Foundation for the Black Experience in Canada

When asked to give an example of a major event in their country's Black history, most Canadians would cite the fact that the Underground Railroad guided enslaved African Americans to freedom within their borders. The Underground Railroad allows Canadians to see their country as the "happy ending" for Blacks, and to view their white ancestors as those who created that happy ending, welcoming those who had suffered under the centuries-old institution of slavery in the New World. It is a straightforward story of the heroic efforts of early Canadians to help a disadvantaged population escape the oppression of a more powerful foe.

What's not to like?

Ever willing to be seen as more enlightened than Americans, Canadians have embraced the story of the Underground Railroad as a prime example of how their society of "peace, order and good government" has done (and by implication, has *always* done) a better job of treating their Black citizens. Canada, not the United States, is clearly the true "land of liberty."

In addition to being "feel good" history and bolstering a positive view of Canada, the Underground Railroad is generally thought to signal the starting point of Canada's Black history. This is a false perception and it has led to a series of assumptions in the general population: Until the mid-nineteenth century, Canada was only home to European settlers and Indigenous peoples. It was always a sanctuary for Blacks. Slavery never existed within the territory that now makes up Canada. "Following the North Star" was always the route to freedom.

As the stories of New Brunswick's Black Loyalists demonstrate, Canada's African founders arrived fifty years earlier than the men and women who escaped slavery via the Underground Railroad. But the Black Loyalists were not the first "Canadians" of African descent; they were simply the country's first *free* Black settlers.

The Europeans who settled in what are now Quebec and Nova Scotia enslaved Africans as labourers and household servants. The earliest enslaved African in Acadia (as Nova Scotia was then known) was Mathieu de Coste, who worked for its French governor in 1608. Slavery was given legal status in New France between 1689 and 1709 when the colony imported Blacks from France to resolve a chronic shortage of labour. New Englanders, who settled in the Maritimes following the Acadian Expulsion of 1755, brought enslaved Africans with them to Halifax, the Annapolis Valley and the St. John River Valley. In 1770, one landowner in Falmouth, Nova Scotia, had no less than sixteen enslaved Blacks.

When the Patriots won the American Revolution, more

than 60,000 Americans who remained loyal to the British Crown became refugees. Seeking sanctuary in what is now Canada, the Loyalists not only provided British North America with tens of thousands of white, English-speaking settlers, they were also the reason for the single largest influx of enslaved people in Canadian history. At one point, the number of Black slaves who accompanied the Loyalists to the Maritimes may have been as high as 2,500.

However, the 60,000-plus Loyalist refugees of the American Revolution also included free Black men and women among their numbers. Later given the name of Black Loyalists, these people had once been the slaves of American rebels. They were granted their freedom in a series of British proclamations on the condition that they escape their masters and then side with the Crown. It was a tactic aimed at destabilizing the Patriot economy and increasing the number of British allies — not a gesture made to abolish slavery. The British did *not* liberate the slaves of white Loyalists.

When the Patriots won the American Revolution, the Black Loyalists joined the evacuation of British troops and loyal American colonists from the new republic. By the end of 1783, between 3,500 and 4,000 Black Loyalists — amounting to one out of every ten Loyalist refugees — had arrived in the colony of Nova Scotia.

Within a year of their arrival, the Loyalist refugees had forced the map of Nova Scotia to be redrawn. The territory that was north of the Bay of Fundy and the Isthmus of Chignecto became the colony of New Brunswick in 1784. Nova Scotia's land mass was further reduced to just its peninsula with the establishment of the colony of Cape Breton Island. Scattered across this redefined corner of the

British Empire were approximately 3,500 *free* Blacks — the Black Loyalist allies of the king.

The history of Canada's free Black settlers begins in the Maritimes. This book examines the lives of nine Black Loyalists who settled in the colony of New Brunswick. Founded by Loyalist refugees, New Brunswick provides us with insights into how late-eighteenth-century American colonists dealt with the completely novel reality of free Blacks living and working in a predominantly white society. It was an unprecedented moment in history — one that could either lay the foundations for a co-operative society in which races were treated with equality or set the template for racist attitudes and institutions that considered one race to be superior to the other.

While it was highly improbable that Loyalist society could ever rise above the systemic racism of the eighteenth century and treat its Black citizens as equals, it was, nevertheless, not beyond the realm of the possible. The story of the early years of New Brunswick's settlement contains a chapter that demonstrates that the colony had the potential to be a genuine land of liberty for its Black settlers. In 1783, the territory that would become New Brunswick was the site of the only known settlement in North America to be founded on abolitionist principles.

In the summer of 1783, forty-nine Quakers gathered in New York City to make plans for a fresh and truly revolutionary start. Forced to become refugees at the end of the War of Independence, those gathered were determined to found a settlement in which every man and woman would truly be free. Whereas American Patriots claimed to have created a land of liberty, the Quaker refugees boldly planned to create the first and only intentional anti-slavery settlement in all of North America.

The newly formed association commissioned three agents to seek out land in western Nova Scotia. When their agents returned with news of a site at Beaver Harbour, 254 refugees boarded the *Camel* and set sail for the mouth of the St. John River. Among their number were eighty Baptists, seven indentured servants and twelve Black Loyalists.

Once they arrived in Belle View, its founders posted a sign at the settlement's entrance: NO SLAVE MASTERS ADMITTED. Here were Loyalists with a vision of a post-revolutionary society that included equality and freedom for all. The Belle View settlement was the only exception to the universal practice of slavery in early Loyalist New Brunswick.

In the years that followed, the settlement at Beaver Harbour swelled to a population of 800. Comprising 15 streets and 149 lots, Belle View was incorporated in 1785. Within five years' time, a forest fire engulfed the town, burning all but one settler's home. The original hope of creating a community of racial equality based upon merchant shipping had not materialized during the settlement's seven-year history. In the aftermath of the fire, Belle View's founders — including its Black Loyalists — decided to seek better opportunities in other settlements along the Bay of Fundy coast.

Belle View's fire destroyed more than buildings; it removed a model of racial equality and harmony that could have served as an example for the rest of New Brunswick, if not for all of British North America. Sadly, it also wiped out any record of the names of its Black Loyalist settlers — men and women who must have carried the memory of equality to other parts of New Brunswick.

Belle View's founders envisioned a society whose basic tenets were far more radical than those of the new republic to the south. But rather than becoming the template for a new kind of racial harmony, the ideals of Belle View were never seriously considered by the rest of the colony's Loyalists. Instead, the colonial leaders felt a more conservative and ordered society would make them the envy of the victorious American Patriots. They envisioned a society that would continue to benefit from the hard labour of Black second-class citizens. Initially given town lots and provisions equal to their white counterparts, the Black Loyalists were helpless to stop the rapid re-establishment of the racist society the white Loyalists had known in the United States.

Within two years of their arrival in New Brunswick, the white majority banned Black Loyalists from working or living within Saint John, the colony's largest city. The city's 1785 charter of incorporation specifically forbade any free Black from living or working within its boundaries unless Saint John's mayor gave that person permission to do so. What would become known as the "Loyalist City" began as a segregated city, intentionally excluding the new colony's Black Loyalists.

While land grants were quickly and generously distributed to white settlers, Blacks had to petition the government to receive equal treatment. Contrary to its American electoral heritage, New Brunswick granted the right to vote to all men whether they owned property or not. However, it did not grant the vote to Black men.

Limited in where they could work, frustrated by the small amount of land they could receive and denied the most basic rights of representation, the Black Loyalists were the first of Canada's founders to suffer from systemic racism. And segregation only gained momentum during the first fifty years of Loyalist settlement in New Brunswick.

When a Black Baptist minister from Nova Scotia visited Saint John in 1790, he risked being imprisoned if he did not receive permission to hold religious services from New Brunswick's Anglican lieutenant-governor. In the end, David George received a certificate to "instruct the Black people in knowledge, and exhort them to the practice of the Christian religion". Although George was free to preach to both whites and Blacks in Nova Scotia, the New Brunswick government made a point of segregating the Christian worshippers within its borders.

White ministers could preach to both white and Black congregations, but in the churches that white Loyalists attended, enslaved Blacks typically sat at the back of the sanctuary. This segregation extended beyond death as well, where, whether free or enslaved, Blacks were either buried at the fringes of white graveyards or laid to rest in an African-only cemetery.

While Black Loyalists had access to the process of petitioning for land and could bequeath property through the probate courts, they were always treated as second-class citizens. Appreciated for skills such as manual labour, housekeeping, cooking and fiddle playing, Blacks were never given the opportunity to demonstrate talents for teaching, community protection and leadership, though they would have the opportunity to do so after their resettlement in Sierra Leone.

When Blacks were mentioned in newspapers in the era of Loyalist settlement, it was only to speak of escaping slaves, the sale of Black slaves, or criminal activity. Newspapers did nothing to remind white Loyalists of the presence of free Blacks who shared the same aspirations for success in the new colony.

Despite these negative perceptions of the Black Loyalists, the community bonds they forged during the American Revolution continued to grow stronger. Free Blacks united to seek land and build their own communities in the early days of New Brunswick settlement. Years of slavery had not quashed the will to succeed or stunted the development of community leaders.

Leaders within the Black Loyalist community generally came from two spheres of life. During the final months of the British occupation of New York City, military authorities had given positions of responsibility to Black men to facilitate the evacuation of loyal refugees. These men were known as "captains" — which was not a rank, but an acknowledgment of their leadership. In the years of settlement in New Brunswick, Black families looked to their former captains to speak on their behalf as they sought land grants from the colonial government. Other leaders became spokesmen for their communities after assuming the position of elders within the colony's Black churches. Seen only as "former slaves," these Black leaders and their demands for equal treatment were usually regarded with disdain by the governing white establishment.

During the first half-century of Loyalist settlement within New Brunswick, the foundations of Canadian anti-Black racism were slowly and inexorably being laid. Despite their records of service during the American Revolution, despite their deep desire to be contributing members of New Brunswick society and despite their shared experiences with white Loyalists, the Black Loyalists were denied the basic rights of British citizenship and were not treated as equals within New Brunswick society.

Always a minority within the larger white society, people

of African descent were continually thwarted in their quest for justice and equality in the centuries that followed Black Loyalist settlement. The Black Refugees — former American slaves granted their freedom by the British during the War of 1812 — were shuffled off into their own communities on the fringes of white settlements. While the "passengers" on the Underground Railroad who found sanctuary in Canada would no longer be considered slaves, they would not be given the same rights as the white colonists.

An interesting but often ignored fact in the story of the Underground Railroad is that the great majority of the fugitive slaves who had found refuge in what is now Ontario returned to the United States at the conclusion of the American Civil War.

As it turned out, Canada was not the land of liberty Blacks had hoped it would be. Black children attended separate schools, Black women were blamed for a rise in prostitution and Black men were held responsible for a rise in crime. Rather than recognizing the racism that prompted Black fugitives to return to the United States, the whites of Ontario and Quebec attributed the departure of their Black neighbours to their difficulties in coping with the severity of the Canadian climate.

In each succeeding era of Canada's history, its Black citizens have had to face a variety of hurdles in their efforts to be treated with justice and equality. And these challenges date back to the eighteenth century, when the first contingent of Black Loyalists arrived in Nova Scotia in the fall of 1782, not to the arrival of the passengers of the Underground Railroad in the nineteenth century.

This book is a starting point in recovering the long-neglected stories of these founding settlers of Canada.

Pushed to the margins of eighteenth-century society, the Black Loyalists of New Brunswick have also had their history shunted to one side. Illiterate through no fault of their own, Black settlers left no diaries, letters or memoirs to shed light on their experiences in the founding of New Brunswick.

Outside of petitions to the colonial government that they dictated to others, there are no historical records that reveal the authentic perspective of the Black Loyalists. Instead, historians have had to draw upon resources created by white Loyalists. Newspapers, probate records, christening rolls, victualling musters and a ledger of Black passengers provide all-too-brief accounts that hint at much richer stories.

Of all the men and women spotlighted in this book, Thomas Peters is the most significant character because of his pivotal role in leading over 200 of New Brunswick's Black Loyalists to Sierra Leone. The stories of the other eight Black Loyalists do not represent a cross section of the experiences of Canada's early African settlers. These men and women would have been largely unknown to New Brunswick's general population during their lifetimes.

Rather than being biographies of famous or typical Black Loyalists, these stories represent the handful of accounts that can be pieced together from available historical resources. Nevertheless, by considering the lives of the Black Loyalists featured in this book, the reader can begin to gain a greater appreciation for what hundreds of Black Loyalists endured as the slaves of American colonists, allies of the British army and refugee founders of New Brunswick.

Within the following pages are the accounts of Thomas Peters and Richard Corankapoon, whose wartime experiences during the American Revolution prepared them to be leaders within New Brunswick's Black Loyalist communities. The reader will also discover how Thomas Hide and others readily appropriated their new rights as British citizens to petition for land, a commodity slaves could never have enjoyed in the United States.

Some Black Loyalists entered into temporary indentures to survive the first difficult years of settlement — an experience that helped establish John Patterson, but proved devastating for Zimri Armstrong. Edward Burr became one of the very few Blacks who acquired enough property to bequeath to his heirs. Facing institutionalized racism and limited opportunities, one Black Loyalist veteran boldly sailed for Britain to seek justice for his people and changed the history of West Africa in the process.

The stories of Black Loyalist women are the most difficult to discover. In the eyes of white society, Blacks were only as valuable as the labour they provided. Not considered equal to whites, their concerns, customs and culture were of little interest to the European majority in North America, whether Patriot or Loyalist. In the eighteenth century, women were generally regarded to have value only as mothers and homemakers. There was little need to educate them beyond the basics as they had no political or economic power and no influence beyond the home. So it is particularly difficult to find accounts of Black women who lived in a society dominated by white men. Beyond references to wives and daughters, this book was able to flesh out the stories of just two Black women: Nancy Mosley, who faced execution for murder, and Cairo Rumsey, an enslaved woman who married a free Black man.

Brief as these biographies may be, they nevertheless outline the challenges and obstacles Black Loyalists confronted in the opening decades of New Brunswick's settlement. They speak of a people who never stopped seeking justice — the first combatants in a struggle that continues to this day as Canadians come to recognize that Black lives *do* matter.

PART ONE:
New Hope in New Brunswick

CHAPTER 1

Thomas Hide: New Brunswick's First Black Loyalist

When the British troop transport ship *Union* sailed into the mouth of the St. John River on May 10, 1783, it was the very first vessel of the spring evacuation fleet to bring Loyalist refugees to what is now New Brunswick. Among its 209 passengers were the first two Black Loyalists to settle in this corner of British North America: a nine-year-old girl named Sukey and a twenty-seven-year-old man named Tom Hide. Both were listed on the *Union*'s manifest as the servants of Fyler Dibblee.

Sukey, a freeborn child, came to New Brunswick as an indentured servant, an arrangement that would provide her with the basic necessities until she reached adulthood. Indentures were a common feature of eighteenth-century society. A person with no resources except for their time and labour signed an indenture contract with an employer, agreeing to work for a set number of years in exchange for shelter, food and clothing. Sometimes the indentured servant might also expect to be trained in a trade or receive a basic education. The system had benefits for both parties. The employee was saved from starvation and homelessness; the employer received a guaranteed source of labour for a set number of years.

It is hard to imagine how a nine-year-old child such as Sukey could have become bound to the Dibblee family as their servant. Parents without enough resources to care for their children often turned to indentures to provide their offspring with the basic necessities. Others sought indentures with craftsmen who could teach their children the skills for a well-paying trade during their years of service. It may well be that Sukey's parents signed her indenture papers with Fyler Dibblee in the belief that they had her best interests at heart.

Sukey would not be the only Black Loyalist indentured to a white Loyalist in the new settlement. Over the next six months, she was followed by twelve other free Blacks who had also decided to indenture themselves to more prosperous refugees.

Tom Hide, on the other hand, was part of a fortunate minority who sailed for New Brunswick as an employee of a white Loyalist. He would not have to spend days or weeks trying to find employment in the rapidly swelling refugee settlements at the mouth of the St. John River. While the disembarked passengers were busy finalizing the location of their lots of land, constructing log cabins and getting used to the routine of receiving food rations from the nearby British garrison, they had little time to establish themselves in the trades they had once pursued in the United States.

With potential white employers still working to set up their businesses, Black Loyalists could not earn wages working in the jobs that had employed them within British lines during the war. During the summer and fall of 1783, the white Loyalists were so preoccupied with building new homes that they were unable to pay for the services of a seamstress, a wagon driver, a laundress, a blacksmith, a chamber maid, a messenger or a cook.

Unlike most Black Loyalists at this time, Tom Hide would be able to earn a living upon his arrival. Fyler Dibblee, his employer, was immediately put to work by the local authorities in his capacity as a lawyer. Dibblee's income meant that Hide would also receive wages. Given time, Hide's next step would be to acquire the thing that authenticated his new status as a free man: his own land.

Until he was twenty-two years old, Hide had been the slave of John Hyde, a Patriot who lived in the town of Fairfield, Connecticut. Hearing of the British promise to emancipate any Patriot's slave who joined the forces of King George III, Tom Hide made his escape to freedom sometime in 1778.

All he had to do was make a twenty-kilometre journey to the safety of the British lines. But despite Fairfield's proximity to freedom and protection, Hide's escape was not an easy one. The nearest British garrison was situated across Long Island Sound. Striking out for Fort Franklin from Connecticut meant venturing into a body of water infested with rebel vessels.

Over the course of the war, Long Island Sound teemed with thousands of small boats ready to pounce on any unsuspecting prey. It could be a ship carrying supplies into New York for the British; it could be a Long Island

Loyalist's vessel bearing goods that could be seized and then resold. If these rebel privateers encountered a runaway slave such as Tom Hide in a boat out on the sound, they could either claim the reward for returning him to his master or sell him for their own gain.

To keep the peace on both land and at sea, more than forty different British units found themselves stationed on Long Island at one time or another over the course of the revolution. The royal army had occupied Long Island since August of 1776, building a series of garrisons to keep the sound safe for British supply ships and to fend off the attacks of rebels based in Connecticut.

Fort Franklin, situated outside of Huntington, was the largest of these garrisons. In addition to the 500 troops stationed there, hundreds of Loyalists from Connecticut and other New England colonies had created a refugee camp just outside Fort Franklin's walls. In leaving slavery in Connecticut, Tom Hide had joined a community of refugees on Long Island.

Whether white or Black, these Loyalists had to fend for themselves within British lines once they escaped violence at the hands of the Patriots. Many earned their living by supporting the king's army: collecting firewood for British headquarters in New York City, foraging for provisions for the troops, or growing crops in the fields of farms abandoned by their rebel owners.

Between 1778 and 1783, Tom Hide was part of a Black Loyalist workforce that was vitally important to the British war effort. The manpower that the Patriots lost due to runaway slaves had become Britain's gain. Black Loyalists such as Hide relieved British soldiers of menial tasks, freeing up the latter to fight on the battlefields of the rebellious colonies. Not having a ready supply of camp followers that would have supported the troops in a European war, the king's army could look to Black Loyalist women to cook, sew, set up tents, deliver messages, nurse, clean clothes and wait on tables. While not permitted to bear arms within the British Army, Black men served the Crown as river pilots, guides and spies. Some were drummers and trumpeters; others worked as wagon drivers and sailors.

With the defeat of the royal army in Yorktown, Virginia, in 1781, the British government lost its will to continue the war and began negotiations to end the American Revolution.

Like other Black Loyalists, Tom Hide wondered if the British would honour their promise to grant protection to the slaves they had emancipated during the war. As American and British negotiators hammered out the terms of the peace treaty to end the revolution, Black and white Loyalists used the time to seek refuge in British strongholds up and down the Atlantic coast, hoping against hope that the Crown would provide evacuation vessels to take them to sanctuary away from the hostile Patriot victors.

Black Loyalists coped with their uncertain future in different ways. Some crowded into New York City, seeking protection from Patriot masters who wanted to enslave them once again. Others tied their fortunes to white refugees who were evacuating the city. They indentured themselves to Loyalists who had made plans to seek refuge in Nova Scotia, Canada, the West Indies and England. Some, like Tom Hide, became the employees of Loyalists.

The circumstances of their meeting are not recorded, but somewhere on Long Island, Tom Hide met Fyler Dibblee, a Loyalist lawyer from Stamford, Connecticut. Recognizing that his wife and six children would need the services of a hired man to construct a home in the wilds of New Brunswick, Dibblee hired the young Black Loyalist sometime before April 1783.

Dibblee was the agent for the *Union*, the flagship of the first fleet of vessels to set sail for western Nova Scotia (today's New Brunswick). He was responsible for keeping an accurate account of the manifest (passengers list) for the evacuation vessel. Like other manifests of this era, it contained columns listing the names of the head of the household, the wife, their children aged ten and older, their children under ten and any servants. Dibblee duly recorded the names of the adult male passengers, but only wrote numbers for entries in the other columns. Despite being Dibblee's employee, Hide's presence on the *Union* was only indicated with a number under the column for "servants."

While this column's title was usually a euphemism for "slaves," it was an entirely accurate description of Tom Hide's legal status. He was a free man employed as a servant by Fyler Dibblee — a status borne out in a ledger known as the *Book of Negroes*.

This ledger had been commissioned by Sir Guy Carleton, the British commander-in-chief for all of North America. As he oversaw the withdrawal of British forces from the new United States of America and organized the evacuation of thousands of Loyalist refugees, Carleton encountered angry Americans who insisted on having their former slaves returned to them.

Although he was not an abolitionist, Carleton nevertheless considered any Black who had supported the British up until November 30, 1782, a free person. Carleton reasoned that since a preliminary peace agreement had been signed on this date, all Blacks who had come within the British lines before that time were free persons and, since they could no longer be described as property, would not be returned to the Patriots who claimed them as such. He reiterated this point in a face-to-face discussion with George Washington in May of 1783, stating that he had no intention of returning any Black who had sided with the British.

So no matter what service was rendered or what age or gender the runaway slaves may have been, they were Black Loyalists and therefore free persons.

To placate the slave owners, Carleton had a ledger created that would record the names and situations of every enslaved African and Black Loyalist who left New York City during the evacuations of 1783. Later, if an American slave owner felt that his property had been taken away on a Loyalist vessel, he could consult the *Book of Negroes* to determine where his slave had gone. As it turned out, the ledger's data was never used to re-enslave Black Loyalists. Carleton's gamble that the process of recapturing a slave would be too much bother had paid off. Although the *Book of Negroes* was a bureaucratic ploy to speed Black Loyalists on their way out of America, it would become a vital document in retelling the stories of emancipated Blacks such as Tom Hide.

To alleviate any anxiety among the Blacks who had trusted the British to grant them their liberty, Carleton had General Samuel Birch, the commandant of New York City, issue certificates to any Black Loyalists who could prove that they had come within British lines by November 1782. Later known as "Birch certificates," these documents guaranteed the bearer the liberty "to go to Nova Scotia or wherever else he may think proper." If a Black Loyalist did not have a Birch certificate or some other document that verified their freedom, they could not board an evacuation vessel.

With his name recorded in the *Book of Negroes* and his Birch certificate in hand, Tom Hide was recognized as a free man. Having served the Crown for five years, he went on board the *Union* as an employee — not a slave — of Fyler Dibblee.

On Thursday, April 24, 1783, the *Union* sailed out of New York harbour. In addition to Tom Hide, the ship was carrying 61 men, 39 women and 108 children. Following the *Union* on its fourteen-day journey to the mouth of the St. John River were nineteen other evacuation vessels that, in total, were transporting 7,000 refugees northward. The spring fleet's fourteen-day journey marked the beginning of the next chapter in Tom Hide's life.

CHAPTER 2
Thomas Hide: The Quest for Land

On May 11, 1783, the *Union* dropped its anchor in the large harbour at the mouth of the St. John River. A small settlement of New England traders hugged the shores, while high up on a rocky hill a small garrison kept watch over the surrounding countryside. For a ship full of refugees whose last view of land had been the buildings of New York City, their new sanctuary seemed to be nothing more than a forest wilderness.

In the weeks that followed their arrival, most of the *Union*'s passengers sought out homes along the St. John River. However, the Dibblee family, their hired man Tom and their indentured servant Sukey settled in Parrtown (Saint John, New Brunswick) on the eastern side of the harbour.

At first, Dibblee's legal skills were in high demand and he was almost immediately appointed to a three-man committee to assess how much land along the St. John River Valley was available for Loyalist settlement. Following his work on the committee that summer, he became a magistrate in Parrtown and one of its agents for refugee settlement.

During Fyler Dibblee's summer absence, Tom Hide and the Dibblees' two teenage sons had the task of constructing the family's log cabin. As was the case for other Loyalist refugees, the Connecticut lawyer had received his land on Parrtown's Prince William Street through a lot draw. Nineteen-year-old Walter and seventeen-year-old William worked alongside Hide while the rest of the family made out as best they could in the canvas army tents provided by the British government.

When the Dibblees' cabin was finished, the furniture the Loyalist family had stored in the hold of the *Union*, including a four poster bed, needed Hide's muscle to put into place. Fyler Dibblee's initial months in Parrtown held the promise of better days to come, prompting him to borrow money from his neighbours. But by that winter he was deep in debt, a financial situation that — in addition to threatening to reduce his family to paupers — meant that the Dibblees could no longer afford to keep Tom Hide as their hired man.

On May 6, 1784, overcome by despair, Fyler died by his own hand. Hide's employer had not been buried a month when a devastating fire swept through Parrtown and burned the Dibblee home to the ground. If the family had not divested itself of its two Black servants during the winter of Fyler's despair, Tom Hide and Sukey were definitely no longer with the Dibblees by the time the authorities granted Fyler's widow land upriver near Kingston.

Sukey, the Dibblees' ten-year-old indentured servant,

disappears from historical records at this point. However, within a year's time, Tom Hide's name, last recorded on a ship's manifest, would reappear on a petition to the New Brunswick government. Following his departure from the Dibblees' employ, Hide had begun to make contacts within the Black Loyalist community in nearby Carleton while he sought work as a labourer.

Along with white Loyalists, a large number of free Blacks were given town lots in Carleton, a community established across the harbour from Parrtown. It did not take long for the Black Loyalists to realize that they could not grow enough food on their minimal lots to sustain their families.

Despite the experiences of privation and persecution they shared with their white neighbours, the Black Loyalists were not treated as equal members of society within their refugee settlements. Although they had escaped slavery in the United States, they could not escape the racism of their era.

In a society that still bought and sold Africans as property, it was difficult, if not impossible, for white Loyalists to perceive free Blacks as anything more than a source of cheap labour. If Tom Hide was going to rise above these perceptions and enjoy life as a free man on his own land, he and his fellow Black Loyalists would have to take matters into their own hands.

In 1785, Carleton and Parrtown were incorporated into the city of Saint John. The new city charter spelled out the status of Black Loyalists in terms no one could fail to understand. It declared that "American and European white inhabitants" could be free citizens of the city and enjoy "all the liberties, privileges and pre-eminences of freemen." (A freeman was someone who had permission to practice his profession within a city.) However, "people of colour or black people . . . are . . . excluded from the privilege of being or becoming free citizens." Furthermore, Blacks were forbidden to work or live within the city limits.

In other words, men such as Tom Hide could not become merchants, tavern keepers, tanners, carpenters, bakers or blacksmiths as white "freemen" could. The very skills that made the Black Loyalists such valuable allies of the British during the American Revolution could not be exercised to aid the empire in the creation of a new colony of loyal Americans.

Barred from life in an urban setting, Black Loyalists' best hope was to receive land along New Brunswick's river valleys where they could establish farms. Two years after arriving in the colony, Tom Hide and eleven other free Black men and their families petitioned the government for land along Belleisle Bay, a tributary of the St. John River near Kingston. He was the seventh man to sign the petition, noteworthy for the fact that it was the only time that he used his full name, Thomas Hide.

In their April 1785 petition, Hide and his companions pointed to the fact that "we have the most of us got large families and [are] destitute of the necessaries of life almost and soon like to be worse without immediate assistance as we are able and willing and desire nothing else but to get our bread by the sweat of our brow."

This was not begging on the part of the Black Loyalists. As with white Loyalists who petitioned for land and better treatment, these men knew that they had earned the right to be heard by the government because of their years of loyal service to the Crown during the American Revolution.

The language of the Black Loyalists' petition demonstrates their understanding of the value of their wartime service. In addressing New Brunswick's lieutenant-governor, Thomas

Carleton (the brother of Sir Guy Carleton, commander-in-chief of the British forces in North America), "his Majesty's loyal subjects" reminded His Excellency that "we came within the British lines as early as 1777 under the sanction of General Howe's proclamation and likewise we were promised by your Excellency's great and good brother Sir Guy Carleton, Commander in Chief of the Royal Army."

Hide and his companions knew their rights as free men and were prepared to appeal to a white government to receive what they were owed. Within just two years of receiving their emancipation certificates, these twelve Black Loyalists began to exercise their rights as free Englishmen. Recognizing what white Loyalists had received in way of provisions and land, the emancipated Africans joined together in a common cause and followed the proper channels to secure the same for themselves.

Although Hide and his compatriots were successful in receiving their land along Belleisle Bay in 1785, the Black Loyalist settlement did not last. A 1788 map of the lower St. John River clearly delineates the location of Black settlements along the Nerepis River and the Long Reach, but there is nothing that indicates a Black community near Belleisle.

How Thomas Hide ended his days remains a mystery. He may have been among the hundreds of Black Loyalists who left New Brunswick for Sierra Leone. In 1791, over 200 of New Brunswick's Black Loyalists responded to the British government's offer of transportation to the coast of West Africa to found a colony of free Blacks. After enduring multiple failed attempts to obtain land in New Brunswick, the prospect of living in a colony of their own was very attractive. However, as the lists of those who left for Africa are incomplete, it is not known if Hide ever considered joining this venture. The colony's first Black Loyalist could have remained in New Brunswick, but there are no colonial probate records, gravestones, church documents or death notices to substantiate this possibility. We know more about how Thomas Hide arrived in New Brunswick in 1783 than how he left it in the decades that followed.

What can be said of Thomas Hide is that at crucial junctures in his life he took action to acquire his basic human rights. When a slave, he took the opportunity offered by the British to become a free man, working alongside other Loyalists throughout the American Revolution. When he found himself on the side of the defeated, he sought out employment, acquired a Birch certificate and became the first Black Loyalist to set foot in New Brunswick. When his employer's suicide forced him to seek out new work, he found employment in Saint John until, with other Black Loyalist petitioners, he was able to acquire his own land along the St. John River.

As the words of his land petition declared, Tom Hide was "able and willing — and desire[d] nothing else but to get our bread by the sweat of our brow."

CHAPTER 3
John Patterson: Eyewitness to History

Though it ended in tragedy, John Patterson's life was a remarkable one. After losing both of his parents, he became part of the largest evacuation of refugees in eighteenth-century North America — the exodus of 60,000 Loyalists who fled the United States. As an adult, he captured New Brunswick's most wanted criminal and his exploits were featured in a book that became a bestseller on both sides of the Atlantic. But more than this, John Patterson had been an eyewitness to the first fifty years of Black Loyalist history in New Brunswick.

Patterson's story begins in New York City, the site of British headquarters throughout the course of the American Revolution. Unlike the hundreds of once-enslaved Blacks who sought refuge in the city, Patterson had not come within the British lines to be set free. He had been born free, a fact that his Black mother and white father had impressed upon him before they died sometime during the revolution. Patterson was in New York City to maintain his freedom.

A Black teenager's insistence that he was free would not mean a great deal to anyone beyond the British-occupied portion of New York. Encompassing Manhattan Island, Staten Island and Long Island, the territory within British lines was the only place in the thirteen rebellious colonies where Blacks' freedom was recognized and protected. Outside of British lines, Patterson faced the very real possibility of being kidnapped and sold as a slave. Staying within New York City was John Patterson's best means of guaranteeing his freedom.

But the city's days as a sanctuary for Blacks were numbered. The Treaty of Paris, which set out the terms of peace to end the American Revolution, included an article that said all runaway slaves were to be returned to their masters. Without anything more than his departed parents' word to validate his claims of being free, Patterson's assertions could quickly be dismissed by the victorious Patriots. He could be seized along with runaways from other colonies and forced into a life of slavery.

During the war, the British had guaranteed Black men and women freedom and protection. The victorious Americans wanted to reverse this change in status and retrieve the men and women they regarded as their property. The Patriots feared that Black Loyalists would be evacuated along with the white Loyalist refugees who sought sanctuary in other parts of the British Empire. Which is, of course, exactly what the British commander-in-chief, Sir Guy Carleton, did when he created the *Book of Negroes* ledger, issued emancipation certificates and evacuated both white and Black Loyalists.

By the spring of 1783, John Patterson was fifteen years old and, without family, needed to make his own plans for the future. While Black adults expected to receive land grants from the British government after leaving the United States, Patterson was still a minor. He was six years too young to receive land. His best hope for survival in Nova Scotia was to become an indentured servant.

Just a month after the first evacuation fleet left New York, Patterson worked out an indenture contract with Charles Loosley, the owner of a popular tavern in nearby Brooklyn. The typical indenture contract required an employer to provide the basic necessities of life (which could include training in a specified trade as well as learning to read and write) in exchange for an employee's unpaid labour for a set number of years. Some indentures lasted for as little as two years while others might end when the employee reached a specified age. Seven years was a very common term of indentured service.

Some indenture contracts were long documents, full of legal jargon and very specific details. Others could be as short as the following contract signed by James White and a girl named Elizabeth Blake in Nova Scotia six years before the Loyalists came to New Brunswick.

> *This Indenture witnesseth that Elizabeth . . . Blake daughter of Mary Blake of Portland, Nova Scotia hath put herself and by these presents, doth voluntarily and with consent of her parent, Mary Blake, put and bind herself apprentice to James White of Portland in Nova Scotia and Elisabeth White, his wife, with them the said James and Elisabeth White, after the manner of apprentice to*

> *serve from the day and date hereof ten years and ten mos. Signed in presence of John Prebel and James Woodman 3rd June* 1777.

No example of an indenture between a white Loyalist employer and a Black Loyalist employee has survived to the present day, but as it was a standard legal procedure, such an indenture would be no different than that entered into by two whites.

For many young, orphaned or widowed supporters of the king, indentures were the only way they could survive their first few years of displacement and settlement. Without a family unit, free Black orphans and widows were not part of households that would receive land from the colonial governments or provisions from the British government. Depending on the work they did as enslaved labourers, some were not suited to farming and felt better able to serve as servants in white Loyalists' homes. According to the *Book of Negroes*, the ledger that listed all of New York City's Black evacuees, John Patterson was one of thirteen Black Loyalists who arrived in New Brunswick as an indentured servant. Many more would enter into indentures in the years that followed.

Patterson was not the only one making plans for life in the northern colony. Charles Loosley had spent his last weeks in New York City gathering up a team of servants to serve as staff for the tavern he planned to open in Parrtown. Travelling with the enterprising bachelor was Isabella, a twenty-six-year-old Black Loyalist woman, her five-year-old daughter and a twenty-eight-year-old man named Jack, all described as "the property of Mr. Loosley."

John Patterson and the rest of Loosley's staff left New York on the *Generous Friends* on the thirteenth of June. They travelled with Company #6, a Loyalist militia led by Thomas Elms, Loosley's former business partner. As it turned out, young John was one of eleven Blacks — both free and enslaved — noted on the ship's passenger list.

The *Generous Friends* dropped anchor at the mouth of the St. John River on the fifth of July. Loosley and his three servants initially settled in Carleton, a community created to accommodate the arrival of thousands of Loyalists. Over the next few months, many other Black Loyalists became their neighbours on the western side of the harbour.

However, it was Parrtown, situated on a peninsula across the harbour from Carleton, that grew to become the largest Loyalist refugee community. Ever sensitive to where the most profit was to be had, Loosley pulled up stakes and built a tavern in the midst of the larger Loyalist settlement. It did not hurt business to have his drinking establishment close to Fort Howe where perpetually thirsty soldiers were garrisoned.

Loosley drew on his experience as a successful tavern keeper in Brooklyn to earn a living for himself and his servants. All it required was good management and a good staff. There was plenty of work for Isabella, Jack and Patterson — serving tables, washing dishes and stocking the shelves with all manner of spirits. Compared to many Black Loyalists who had become indentured servants, John Patterson was lucky to have found work that kept him indoors, out of the elements, and did not require backbreaking physical labour.

But the refugee settlement had dangers other than the frigid climate and the rigours of the wilderness. On June 18, 1784, a devastating fire swept through Parrtown, destroying newly built log cabins and the few possessions the Loyalists had brought with them. The community had barely recovered from the first conflagration when, in November, a second fire consumed more of Parrtown.

Rather than risking the loss of another tavern to a third fire, Loosley sought better prospects outside of New Brunswick. He took John Patterson and his other servants to the Loyalist boomtown of Shelburne, Nova Scotia, which at this time was the fourth largest city in all of North America.

Living in Shelburne was a very different experience for Patterson. During his off-hours, the seventeen-year-old had the opportunity to meet the settlers of nearby Birchtown, the largest community of free Blacks in the world outside of Africa. It was a once in a lifetime experience. Never again would Patterson be surrounded by so many people of African descent.

Although Shelburne did not experience the destructive fires that had levelled Parrtown, it nevertheless went through a long and lingering decline as both Black and white Loyalists discovered its promised prosperity was founded on nothing more than wishful hopes and dreams. In the face of diminishing profits, Charles Loosley closed his tavern, gathered up his staff and returned to New Brunswick. If the Loyalist innkeeper could not make a living upon his return, divesting himself of his assets would be a prudent move — assets that included the indenture agreement with John Patterson.

Rather than setting up shop in the newly incorporated city of Saint John (an amalgamation of Carleton and Parrtown), Loosley decided to open his third tavern further up the St. John River. In January of 1789, the *Royal Gazette* and the *New Brunswick Advertiser* carried an advertisement that informed the public that Charles Loosley was now in business in Grimross (modern Gagetown) in a "good stately looking home, rather unfinished but comfortable" where the public could enjoy good food, good drink and comfortable beds. His inn had warm stables for horses as well as oats and English hay "at moderate prices as usual." Though not mentioned in the ad, John Patterson, now twenty-one years old, was part of the tavern's staff that anticipated serving the colony's travelling public.

Loosley had positioned his new inn on the St. John River about two-thirds of the way between Saint John and Fredericton. While John Patterson washed tables, tended horses and worked around Loosley's inn, he was able to keep abreast of news from all over the colony from the travellers who stopped in at the tavern.

Slavery was still a fact of life in New Brunswick; some of Loosley's most prosperous neighbours in Grimross had enslaved Blacks to tend the fields on their growing estates. Rather than maintaining poor-houses to feed and shelter the colony's disadvantaged citizens, the New Brunswick government legislated that indentures were the best way to cope with unemployment among the poor. Given their treatment within the colony's racist social structure, many Black Loyalists who had been unable to find paying jobs were forced to enter into indentured service.

When Saint John's 1785 charter forbid "people of colour or black people" to work within the city following its incorporation, enterprising Blacks followed the example of white Loyalists and petitioned the government for land in the colony's interior. Consequently, by the time John Patterson was waiting on tables in Grimross, a number of Black Loyalist communities had grown up. There were settlements on both sides of the Long Reach, along the Nerepis River near Westfield, in nearby Fredericton, Otnabog and Maugerville as well as in Quaco along the Fundy coast.

However positive these developments might have seemed, there was a great deal of frustration within Black Loyalist communities. Eight years after their arrival in New Brunswick, a hundred Black families described themselves as "destitute and helpless" as they waited for the land the British government had promised them. The injustices they had endured at the hands of New Brunswick's colonial government prompted Thomas Peters, a Revolutionary War veteran, to act. Charged with representing "their unhappy situation," Thomas sailed to London to make a personal appeal for more land and greater equality.

When he returned in October of 1791, Peters brought news of a fresh start for New Brunswick's beleaguered Blacks — the opportunity to found a colony of their own in Sierra Leone. Within two months' time, over 200 Black Loyalists had boarded ships in Saint John and bid farewell to New Brunswick.

While the Sierra Leone exodus included many from the Black communities established along the St. John River, it could not include John Patterson. To qualify for settlement in the West African colony, applicants had to be debt-free, law-abiding free Blacks. Indentured servants or slaves need not apply. The strategy that had provided Patterson with shelter, food and clothing following his flight from America now prevented him from taking advantage of a fresh start in Africa. At twenty-three years of age, Patterson remained Charles Loosley's indentured servant with no choice but to stay in New Brunswick.

The historical records do not pinpoint the year John Patterson finally completed his indenture. What is known is that after becoming a free man, he left Grimross and settled on land in York County, just outside of Fredericton.

It would not be until 1814 that Patterson's name would once again appear in the public record, this time not as a tavern keeper's servant but as a forty-six-year-old farmer.

In 1814 a New Brunswick court convicted Henry More Smith of the capital offense of horse stealing. Incarcerated in the county prison in Kingston, Smith was to remain there until the date of his hanging. But, despite the watchful eyes of Sheriff Walter Bates and his jailer, Smith managed to escape. He wasted no time in making his way north along the St. John River in the hope of crossing into the United States and out of the reach of the New Brunswick justice system.

Thomas Wetmore, the colony's attorney general, immediately posted a fifty-dollar reward for Smith's capture — and then raised it to eighty dollars. Although Smith was apprehended just before he reached the American border, his captors were not able to claim the reward money. Ever the escape artist, Smith eluded his captors and once again stole a horse.

Within a few days, Smith discovered an ideal hiding spot, described as a "barrack," just three kilometres outside of Fredericton. As it turned out, Smith had hidden himself and his horse in the small hay barn that belonged to John Patterson.

At first, Patterson was completely unaware of Smith's presence in his barrack or of the fugitive's raids on the good citizens of Fredericton. Over several nights, Smith had used the Black Loyalist's farm as his base for a series of daring thefts in the capital city. One evening, Smith brazenly entered the home of Thomas Wetmore, the attorney general who, weeks earlier, had posted a reward for his capture. As guests dined at Wetmore's table, Smith stole their coats and dashed back to his hideout. There, he hid himself beneath the Black Loyalist's hay and remained out of sight during the day.

Smith's best-laid plans started to unravel when Patterson paid a visit to his hay barn and noticed that things were not as he had left them. Moving a pile of hay to one side, Patterson found Smith asleep with a white scarf wrapped around his neck. When awakened, Smith quickly made up a story, saying that he was from the Kennebecasis River and was in the Fredericton area in the hopes of buying land. He apologized profusely to the Black farmer for any harm done to his hay.

Suspicious, Patterson decided to take Smith at his word for the moment and allowed him stay in the barn. But the Black Loyalist kept a watchful eye on his "mysterious stranger." When Patterson spied Smith climbing out of the barrack's window and heading for the woods, he became convinced that his suspicious visitor must be a deserter from the British army. Patterson quickly formed his neighbours into a posse and went off in pursuit of Smith. When he captured the fugitive thief, he promptly delivered him to the sheriff in Fredericton.

As he headed back to his farm, Patterson remembered that Smith was not wearing his white scarf when he was put in jail. The Black Loyalist returned to his barrack to see if Smith's scarf had been left behind in the hay. There, to his surprise, Patterson discovered all the coats Smith had stolen from the attorney general's dinner guests. Patterson carried the coats back to Fredericton where they were returned to their proper owners.

The Fredericton judge then ordered that Smith be returned to the custody of Walter Bates, the Kings County sheriff. Until Bates arrived, the judge wisely shackled Smith in handcuffs and an iron collar secured by a ten-foot chain. Patterson, meanwhile, remained in Fredericton to claim the reward for Smith's capture.

When Bates arrived by sloop to take Henry Smith on the ninety-kilometre river voyage back to Kingston, John Patterson accompanied him, holding Smith's chain to ensure that he did not escape the sheriff once again.

By midnight on the thirtieth of October, Bates had locked Smith away in the Kings County jail. As he gave John Patterson the reward advertised for the capture of New Brunswick's most wanted criminal, Bates thanked the Black Loyalist for all of his efforts to bring Smith to justice.

How Patterson spent the eighty-dollar reward goes unrecorded.

Walter Bates, the Kingston sheriff, decided that the story of Henry More Smith had enough twists and turns in it to make an interesting book. Within three years of John Patterson's capture of Smith, Bates sent his manuscript to a Connecticut publisher. *The Mysterious Stranger* went on to become the first international bestseller written by a Loyalist. Completely oblivious to the success of Bates's book, John Patterson had no way of knowing that his role as a bounty hunter was being read by thousands on both sides of the Atlantic. Henry Smith, the "stranger" referenced in the book's title, was eventually pardoned for his various crimes and left New Brunswick, never to return.

Unaware of his moment in history's spotlight, Patterson continued to work on his farm outside of Fredericton. A year after the capture of Smith, New Brunswick received its second influx of refugees of African descent. Granted their freedom because they had sided with the British during the War of 1812, 300 emancipated slaves arrived in Saint John on June 8, 1815. While many settled to the east of the city in Loch Lomond, others made homes in Otnabog near Grimross or in Kingsclear, just above Fredericton.

In 1816, the York County Roll Book included John Patterson in its census records, listing his occupation as "a labourer." This may have simply been a convenient label to describe Patterson's work as a farmer — but it might also indicate that the Black Loyalist had abandoned or sold his farm to pursue other work. No records of the era shed light on whether Patterson was married or had any children.

The last reference to John Patterson is a tragic one found in the *New Brunswick Royal Gazette*. In just a few sentences, the Fredericton newspaper reported on an inquest into the death of John Patterson, a "coloured man" who had spent the night of April 24, 1833, with the Staples family. They had allowed the sixty-five-year-old Patterson to sleep near their fireplace for the night. At five o'clock on the following morning, the Staples's servant discovered the old Black Loyalist, "his body very burnt, his clothes having taken fire by some accident during the night. Died two hours later."

For a Black Loyalist to have his name noted just once in the historical records is significant; the fact that we know anything more about John Patterson after he left New York City in 1783 is truly remarkable. His life, both tragic and triumphant, encompassed the first fifty years of Black Loyalist history in New Brunswick, making him an eyewitness to the founding of the colony, its opportunities and injustices and the formation of its first Black communities.

CHAPTER 4
Pompey Rumsey and Cairo: A Black Loyalist Love Story

The lives of Black Loyalists must be pieced together from documents scattered over time and space. A prime example is the story of Pompey Rumsey and Cairo, which is told through just four sources: a letter, a ledger's entry, a probate record and a church's christening register.

Their story begins with the arrival of Sir Guy Carleton in New York City in April of 1783. Much to his chagrin, Carleton had been appointed the commander-in-chief of British forces in North America. His assignment held out no promise of military glory. Instead, he was given the unenviable task of overseeing the evacuation of British troops and Loyalist refugees from New York City before peace was officially declared between the United States and the United Kingdom. The treaty that set out the conditions of Britain's surrender at the end of the American Revolution would take effect in September.

Within that five month time span, Carleton had to fulfill the onerous job description that had been given him by Lord North, King George III's new secretary of state. In a letter to Carleton, North said the he was to "remain at New York till the principal arrangements are settled, which are necessary for the speedy and orderly execution of the great and complicated business which you have now in hand. The removal and destination of the troops under your command, the security and disposal of the public property, the proper regulations for the liquidation and adjustment of the accounts, the care, support and assistance to be afforded to the Loyalists, are but a few of the points which will come under your consideration."

In addition to delegating these tasks to a team of officers and civil servants, Carleton also needed to hire the staff necessary to oversee his household during his temporary stay in New York City. One of those hired was a free Black man named Pompey Rumsey. In a city that was transitioning from seven years as the nerve centre of British operations during the war, Rumsey had secured a position that many could only dream of. Working for the highest-ranking British officer in North America gave Rumsey a job with a good salary, providing him with clothing, food and shelter of the highest standard.

His job also brought Rumsey into contact with British officers, the members of New York's social elite and prominent Patriot leaders when they visited the commander-in-chief at his home. Such visitors would bring with them their own entourage of servants and slaves, giving Rumsey the opportunity to meet others of African descent. While Carleton conferred with his military staff, heard the concerns of Loyalist refugees and negotiated with

American politicians, the Black maids, coachmen, drivers and manservants who had been brought together by these matters of state exchanged gossip and forged social contacts.

One of the visitors to Carleton's home was James Peters, a Loyalist from Long Island. After this ardent British supporter sought sanctuary within New York City in 1782, the commander-in-chief made Peters one of seven agents responsible for settling Loyalist refugees in Nova Scotia. Among the members of Peters's household staff who had relocated to New York was a nineteen-year-old slave girl named Cairo.

The meeting of Pompey Rumsey and Cairo was of little consequence to either Sir Guy Carleton or James Peters; the latter were too busy working out the details of the massive refugee evacuation to the St. John River. As Carleton and his Loyalist agents made their plans, Pompey and Cairo fell in love and were married.

Despite the potential for separation at the whim of slave owners, marriages between enslaved and free Blacks were not uncommon at this time. Nevertheless, Pompey and Cairo had taken a great risk. There was always the danger that Cairo would be separated from Pompey if he could not buy her freedom or if her master did not set her at liberty. As "property," an enslaved wife such as Cairo had no rights and was compelled to go wherever her master went. The fate of the Rumseys' marriage lay in the choices made by Cairo's master, James Peters.

In April of 1783, the first fleet of Loyalist evacuees set sail for the mouth of the St. John River. Among them was James Peters, who had booked passage on the *Sovereign*. The Loyalist agent had left his family and servants back in New York while he applied himself to his new tasks. As Cairo helped Margaret Peters prepare for the family's trip north, James Peters oversaw the assignment of land to the hundreds of Loyalists pouring into what was then northwestern Nova Scotia. The most equitable method was to have the refugees receive their land through a drawing of lots.

Since the first landfall for the Loyalists was the area surrounding the harbour that connected the Bay of Fundy to the St. John River, it was the first to be divided into lots. White Loyalists initially drew lots in either Carleton on the harbour's west side or in Parrtown on the east side. Black Loyalists drew lots in Carleton.

After spending the summer supervising the distribution of Loyalist land, Peters returned to New York City in September to report to Sir Guy Carleton. In Peters's absence, his wife, Margaret, and their Black slaves had been packing up their worldly goods and preparing their young family for the move to the St. John River.

In early October, Peters, his wife, their five children and their three enslaved Blacks had been assigned accommodations on board the *Alexander*. Their departure date was set for Tuesday, the seventh of October. It is not known how long James and Margaret Peters had been aware of Cairo's marriage to Pompey Rumsey, but whether it had been months or days, they did nothing to alleviate Cairo's fear of being separated from her husband until just before the *Alexander* set sail.

As the day of the Peters's departure drew closer, Rumsey approached Cairo's master. He was more than willing to leave New York with Cairo, but he had to be released from his position within Carleton's household — and he needed official documentation to prove that he was not the property of an American slave owner.

Rather than going to Sir Guy Carleton in person, James Peters sent him a "memorial," a formal request for a favour from the commander-in-chief. In his letter, Peters bluntly explained the situation: "A Negro named Pomp in His Excellency's family" was married to one of Peters's slaves. This domestic situation was rather awkward as Peters was "going to Nova Scotia with his family." Speaking of Rumsey, Peters wrote, "the said Negro has expressed a desire of going with his wife," and so the question was raised as to whether he "may accompany his wife and be furnished with a passport."

While the records of Carleton's correspondence during his time in New York do not reveal his answer to James Peters's request, the *Book of Negroes* ledger does. Commissioned to record the names and circumstances of every free and enslaved Black leaving the port of New York in 1783, the ledger duly noted the six Africans who sailed aboard the *Alexander* on the seventh of October. At the head of the list was twenty-year-old Cairo and fourteen-year-old Bella, who were both the property of James Peters. They were followed by the names of another Loyalist's two slaves, a free Black and then, "Pompey, 25, stout fellow, on his own bottom. Born free."

Sir Guy Carleton had, in the end, dismissed Rumsey, provided him with the needed documentation and sent him on his way. Pompey Rumsey had left the employ of the most prominent man in New York City to stay by his enslaved wife's side. Having left the United States "on his own bottom" — that is, as a free man — Pompey's life was now tethered to that of the family who considered his wife their property.

During the five decades that followed the arrival of the Loyalists, enslaved Africans were considered as little more than livestock. Advertisements from this era indicate that white New Brunswickers sold slaves at prices ranging from twenty-five to forty pounds, depending on their age and ability to work. Just three years after the Rumsey couple arrived in New Brunswick, the colony's *Royal Gazette* carried the advertisement of "A Negro boy for sale." The last known sale of a slave in New Brunswick appeared in the same newspaper on October 16, 1809, when a Loyalist advertised one of his Negro women, guaranteeing a "good title" to any purchaser. Had he been so inclined, James Peters could have sold Cairo Rumsey in like manner.

After initially settling on their town lot in Parrtown, the Peters family moved upriver to Grimross (Gagetown) where they had received a grant of 360 acres. This would be home for Pompey and Cairo for the rest of their lives.

Over the years, James Peters established two farms, each with its own grand house. "Glenora" was built on the highlands while the "Mount House" was located on Peters's valley land. In addition to all of the responsibilities for overseeing so many households, Margaret gave birth to three more children after the couple made their home in Grimross.

With eight children to supervise and two separate farms to manage, the Peters required more slave labour than Pompey, Cairo and their initial set of "servants" could provide. After establishing his estate, Peters bought at least three more Africans to work on his farm and in his home. A 1799 newspaper ad offered a reward for the recapture of two Black slaves named Gill and Dick — one of whom was the property of James Peters. When Peters wrote up a will in 1806, he made reference to a second slave: "my Negro man Len." Eliza Fisher, a slave from Virginia, entered into service on the Peters farm as a four-year-old. She stayed with the family until she was nineteen.

As can be seen, slavery was all too prevalent in New Brunswick during the early decades of Loyalist settlement. Enslaved Africans were among the first to arrive in the colony. Known as the Spring Fleet, the first twenty Loyalist evacuation vessels that set sail for the mouth of the St. John River in April of 1783 had nine slaves among their passengers. By the fall, no less than 129 enslaved Blacks were working to help their white masters establish homes in the wilderness of the St. John River valley or at Parrtown.

The second New Brunswick destination for enslaved Blacks was Fort Cumberland, the site of modern day Aulac, near the border between Nova Scotia and New Brunswick. While they were only ten in total, they represented two out of every three Blacks who were brought to this region. It would be very difficult for the five free Black Loyalists who disembarked from the *Trepassey* in October of 1783 to be treated as British citizens given that so many of their brethren were considered the property of their white neighbours.

Forty-three of the ships that carried white Loyalists to New Brunswick had slaves as their passengers. The ledger listed 139 slaves with 89 different Loyalist masters brought to (what would become) New Brunswick. However, these are only the ships that are registered in the *Book of Negroes*. Although this ledger was to serve as a record of all free and enslaved Blacks who left New York City, it was not a complete or exhaustive list. Some Loyalists hired their own evacuation ships; others arrived in New Brunswick after 1783. In other words, the 139 slaves recorded in the *Book of Negroes* as arriving in New Brunswick can only be understood to represent the *minimum* number of enslaved Blacks brought to the colony.

By the spring of 1784, just a year after the *Book of Negroes* was compiled, a muster of Loyalists living on the St. John River listed 441 "servants," who, for the most part, would have been of African descent and enslaved. That same year, a military return determined that 444 slaves had arrived in what would soon become the colony of New Brunswick. This number grew even larger when several slave owners from Nova Scotia decided to relocate to the newly created colony. In total, it is estimated that the Loyalists brought more than 1,230 slaves into the Maritimes immediately following the American Revolution.

An example of a slave brought to New Brunswick who was not recorded in the *Book of Negroes* or the military return is found in a news item in the August 30, 1862, issue of the *Carleton Sentinel*. A "coloured man" named Moses Hodges, who was known to be over a hundred years of age, had died a few days earlier. The *Sentinel* went on to report that "he came to the province with one of the loyalist families in 1776 having been a slave previous to that on a southern plantation."

A quick review of the early probate records reveals more names of enslaved Blacks and their white Loyalist slave owners. Benjamin Seaman, who died in Saint John in 1785, bequeathed his "Negro boy called Will" along with his watch, cane, gun and sword to his son William. His second son John received his "Negro boy called Tom."

A year later, the Rev. John Sayre, an Anglican priest, died and left a variety of items to his wife and son. However, this Connecticut Loyalist made a provision in his will that his "servant Rosanna be freed." Rosanna did better than most slaves. In 1789, when an inventory was made of the estate of Richard Hewlett, it included £336 of goods as well as "one Negro boy" valued at twenty-five pounds. No provisions were made for his emancipation.

In the spring of 1796, the will of New York Loyalist Samuel Hallett provided his wife with furniture, a large mirror, all the paintings in their home and "a Negro woman named Phillis." Four years later, a Loyalist from New Jersey named Charles Harrison divided up his worldly possessions among his children, including his "old servant Negro." The latter was not identified by name but was, instead, noted for his monetary value — ten pounds.

Jacob Ellegood was a Loyalist from Virginia who was used to having a great number of enslaved Africans. At his death in 1802, his son William received "all my Negroes except one wench called Betty and one girl not above 12 years of age." His granddaughter Rebecca was willed "one Negro girl not above 12 years of age to be chosen by her." His son Jacob Junior was to receive his "Negro boy John." His son John was to be granted his "mulatto wench Pleasant and her three children, James, Sally and William." Finally, his son Samuel Ellegood was to be given a slave referred to as his "Negro boy Irvin."

When John Hume, a Loyalist who settled in Westfield, New Brunswick, died in 1804, his will revealed that he once worked as a mason in the West Indies with "his two Negroes." He must have brought his two skilled slaves to New Brunswick with him, as there was a further reference to Hume doing stonework in May of 1785 with "three Negro masons."

George Harding died in Maugerville in 1808, leaving his daughter Elizabeth Miles "all livestock and all Negro slaves." A year later, the Rev. James Scovil left a third of all his real estate and his "two servant boys Robert and Sampson" to his wife, Amy. The term "servant" clearly meant "slave" as Scovil instructed that the two Blacks be "set at liberty" on their twenty-sixth birthdays, "provided they do faithfully discharge the duty of servants until that period."

Robert was twelve and Sampson was ten years old when the will was written in 1804 — evidence that Scovil had bought the boys *after* his arrival in New Brunswick. The colony's slaves were not simply "property" the Loyalists had brought with them in 1783, they also included those purchased in a slave trade that continued for decades after the founding of New Brunswick. After the death of Rev. Scovil in 1809, Robert would have had to wait nine years for emancipation and Sampson would have had to endure eleven more years of enslavement before he was set free.

As these wills show, the white Loyalists who enslaved Blacks usually had only one or two in their household. The largest number of slaves belonging to a Loyalist in New Brunswick were the seven owned by Isaac Allen, a future judge of the colony's supreme court.

Coming from the American colonies, where slave labour was crucial to the success of large plantations or the maintenance of an estate, white Loyalists such as James Peters were utterly dependent on the services of slaves such as Cairo Rumsey and those that were purchased following the family's arrival in New Brunswick. Their services allowed the New York Loyalist time for other pursuits in the growing colony.

After he established his estates in Grimross, Peters became the First Magistrate of Queen's County, a Justice of the Peace, a Justice of the Inferior Court of Common Pleas, a member of New Brunswick's House of Assembly, the Registrar of Deeds and Wills, a vestryman in the local Anglican Church and a lieutenant-colonel in the county militia.

When, in 1791, New Brunswick's Black population was given the opportunity to found a colony of free men and women in Sierra Leone, West Africa, Cairo Rumsey could not even consider this possibility because of her status as a slave. Pompey, her husband of eight years, could have abandoned her and sailed for Sierra Leone to enjoy his full potential as a free man, but, as he had done in New York, Pompey once again chose to forfeit his rights as a Black Loyalist and remained with his enslaved wife.

At sixty years of age, James Peters composed a handwritten will. As well as outlining his intentions for the distribution of his possessions, it provides an insight into the lives of Pompey and Cairo Rumsey twenty-three years after their arrival in New Brunswick. Despite Cairo's long years of service to the family, her master's will did not promise to set her at liberty upon Peters's death. Instead, Peters instructed that Cairo should live with his wife, Margaret, and serve her as long as she remained a widow.

If Margaret remarried, Cairo was given a choice "in consideration of her long and faithful service": She could continue to live with Margaret or she could live with one of Peters's eight children. The Loyalist further informed his heirs that he wanted Cairo to "be kindly treated and provided with every necessary that may contribute to render her comfortable and happy in her declining years." (Cairo was forty-three years old when her master wrote this will in 1806.)

While this regard for Cairo may seem generous on Peters's part, he could have been more generous; two lines later in the will, he asks that his "Negro man Len" be manumitted (set free). Although he was neither Peters's property nor responsibility, Pompey Rumsey also appeared in the Loyalist's 1806 will. Peters asked that Cairo's forty-eight-year-old husband "be kindly treated and provided for if required." How these terms were carried out is not known. Peters did not die until 1820, thirteen years after making known his intentions for his human property.

In 1807, the year after Peters first composed his will, the British government passed the *Act of Parliament* that abolished the slave trade throughout its empire — although it would be almost twenty-five years before slavery itself came to an end, on August 28, 1833. Five years later, every slave within the British Empire had finally been set at liberty. If the Rumseys had lived to see this day, Cairo would have been seventy and Pompey, seventy-five.

There are no records to indicate whether or not Pompey and Cairo had children of their own. However, the evidence found in local christening records demonstrates that their lives had left a positive impact on at least one family in their community. While we do not know when the Rumseys died, both of their names lived on for one more generation through another Black family's children.

The baptismal records for St. John's Anglican Church in Gagetown contain the last known historical references to the Black Loyalist and his enslaved wife. Among the children baptized in early 1822 was the second daughter of Richard and Sarah Hopewell. The Hopewells were Black farmers who lived near the Peters's estate. In fact, the Hopewells were so well acquainted with the white Loyalist family that Valentine, the Peters's oldest son, served as a witness at their wedding. The Hopewells had their daughter christened Cairo Rumsey Hopewell. Three years later, they named their son John Pompey Rumsey Hopewell. Their names would be the only legacy the Black Loyalist and his wife had to leave to New Brunswick's next generation of Blacks.

In choosing to marry an enslaved woman, Pompey Rumsey lost the opportunity to plot his life's course, the possibility of owning land and the provisions offered to other Black Loyalists. He could not seek employment in urban centres such as Fredericton or Saint John and he could not consider the opportunity of moving to Sierra Leone. Pompey's devotion to his wife not only speaks well of his character, but testifies to what a remarkable woman Cairo must have been.

CHAPTER 5
Nancy Mosley: A Black Loyalist on Trial

In the late eighteenth century, only two occasions in a woman's life would bring her to public notice in a dignified manner: the announcement of her wedding and the notice of her death. In both cases, it was her relationship to a prominent man that would earn her this brief moment in the spotlight. There was only one other means by which a woman would come to public attention — and this one was considerably less dignified: scandal, whether marital or criminal.

Nancy Mosley was no exception. The Black Loyalist woman achieved notoriety as the prime suspect in New Brunswick's very first murder trial. The alleged instrument of death: an iron table fork worth six pence.

Nancy's story began like that of the hundreds of other Black Loyalist women who found sanctuary in New Brunswick following the American Revolution. Nancy seized the opportunity offered by the British and ran away from her rebel master. Not the least of the consequences for this desperate gamble, should she be recaptured, was the possibility of a violent whipping. But she took the risk.

Once within the British lines, Nancy was put to work supporting the British war effort. While Black Loyalist women did not bear arms, they nevertheless provided a variety of valuable services that improved the quality of day-to-day life for the British and German troops who were fighting American rebels. In a traditional European war, armies relied on soldiers' wives and unmarried camp followers to do all of the things necessary to support the troops when they were off the battlefield. Without access to a large pool of female labour in North America, the British army valued the role of Black Loyalist women such as Nancy.

Some women worked as seamstresses, repairing uniforms and canvas tents, while others were employed to launder soldiers' clothing. Black Loyalist women cooked, fetched water, collected firewood, worked as orderlies in military hospitals or served as messengers. When the British forces occupied rebel towns and cities, free Blacks saw to the domestic needs of the king's officers. The tasks that these women had been compelled to do as the chattel of American rebels now became the means of securing their freedom once the war came to an end.

At some point, Nancy made her way north to New York City. After she arrived on Manhattan Island, Nancy encountered thousands of other Black Loyalists — men, women and children who had run away from their rebel masters. Coming from a variety of backgrounds, these fugitive slaves were now rubbing shoulders with the largest numbers of Africans they had encountered since their arrival in America. Nancy's work would bring her into contact with Blacks who had escaped slavery from New Hampshire to Georgia. Having worked from the plantations in the south to the seaports of New England, these Black Loyalists brought a variety of work experiences and skills to aid the British cause. Nancy would also encounter Africans who came from a variety of ethnic heritages and languages. But despite their differences, Black Loyalists began to forge new friendships and support groups as they worked together in New York. Later, they would use these new social connections as the basis for their lives as free men and women.

Unrestrained by the limited social life that slavery had once imposed, Nancy now had the opportunity to meet eligible Black men. They served the British as carpenters, teamsters, blacksmiths, regimental drummers, butchers and sailors. One Black Loyalist, John Mosley by name, gained her affections and asked to be her husband. By the summer of 1783, Nancy had married John Mosley and given birth to their first child.

Events far from New York City determined the next chapter in the lives of the Mosley family. Following the victory of the American forces at the Battle of Yorktown on October 19, 1781, the British government began to negotiate the terms of a peace treaty. The Americans considered the thousands of Blacks who had sided with the British during the war to be nothing more than stolen property. During the negotiations with the British delegates, they insisted that the peace treaty should contain a clause that would require all former slaves to be returned to their masters. Anticipating the treaty, rebel enslavers began to arrive in New York City in early 1783 to recapture Black Loyalists such as John and Nancy Mosley.

It was a time of uncertainty and dread for the young couple. Boston King, one of their fellow Blacks, would later recall seeing rebels "seizing upon their slaves in the streets of New York, or even dragging them out of their beds."

The threat of recapture meant more than simply the loss of Nancy's individual freedom: she would also be forever separated from her husband, John. The fate of Nancy's child would be even more tragic. Having been born within British lines, the Mosley child was free. With Nancy's capture, the child would not only be taken from their father, but would also be forced into slavery with their mother.

Fortunately for Nancy and John, the British commander-in-chief in New York City had his own interpretation of the peace treaty's clause regarding the return of American slaves. Sir Guy Carleton argued that any Black who had come within the British lines by the end of 1782 was a free person and had been recognized as such by the British government. Since they had been emancipated by the Crown, Carleton reasoned that Black Loyalists were no longer the property of American slave owners and therefore would not be returned to their former masters. They would be treated the same as white Loyalists and given sanctuary in other parts of the British Empire.

To further legitimize the new status of the Black Loyalists, Carleton began to issue certificates that officially recognized the freedom that had been granted by the Crown during the revolution. Signed by one of two commandants in charge of troop and civilian evacuations, these documents became known as Birch certificates and Musgrave certificates.

Once Nancy and John Mosley learned how the British planned to help them leave the United States, they went before the newly struck British-American Board of Inquiry. The board, which included New York City's British commandant and a group of American and British officials, interviewed former slaves at Fraunces' Tavern every Wednesday from April to November of 1783. The application process, sometimes referred to as a Birch trial, judged each Black on the testimony they offered as evidence of their loyal service.

Once recognized as free persons, John and Nancy Mosley then received their certificates — a single piece of paper declaring that the bearer could "go to Nova Scotia, or wherever else he may think proper." It is little wonder that a Black Loyalist would later write that receiving his Birch certificate "dispelled all our fears and filled us with joy and gratitude."

Although no ship was allowed to carry Black passengers out of New York City unless their names were recorded in the *Book of Negroes* — with ship captains facing severe punishment and the responsibility of returning unlisted Blacks to New York City — John and Nancy Mosley's names are not recorded there. So how did they make it to New Brunswick? In April of 1783, a sloop and a schooner defied the regulations, leaving New York without being examined. It is more than likely that the Mosleys were among the Black refugees who sailed for Nova Scotia aboard one of these vessels.

The journey from New York City to Nova Scotia usually took about two weeks to complete and it was not without its dangers. A refugee evacuation vessel might encounter hostile American privateers who would consider any Black passengers as goods to be captured and sold. Crowded conditions on board the ships often provided the breeding ground for a variety of deadly diseases. The forces of nature also claimed their share of evacuation vessels. There was the ever-present danger of a storm at sea that might capsize a ship or drive it off course. The powerful tides of the Bay of Fundy and the rocky shoals of Nova Scotia's coastline had been the cause of a number of shipwrecks, so Black Loyalists were not truly safe from danger until their vessel dropped anchor at its destination.

In the case of the Mosleys, that destination was Parrtown. Upon their arrival, the Mosleys' first task was to build some sort of shelter. John had two choices: join other Loyalist refugees in cutting down the trees that surrounded Parrtown to build a log cabin for Nancy and their child, or take advantage of the offer of old canvas tents provided by the British army.

Across the harbour to the west of Parrtown was the new settlement of Carleton, named in honour of the British commander-in-chief. Whether by design or because of the positive regard that Black Loyalists held for Sir Guy Carleton, this area was largely settled by free Blacks. However, John Mosley drew a lot for a land grant on the Parrtown peninsula in an area that was known as the Lower Cove. His lot, #1084, was located on Stormont Street (today's St. James Street, just a block south of Queen Square). Given the abundance of trees on his lot, John built a log cabin as his family's first home.

For the next twelve months, the Mosleys would be supplied with food and provisions from Fort Howe, the British garrison that guarded the mouth of the St. John River. The garrison's commissariat, usually responsible for feeding the soldiers who were stationed at the fort, now had the added responsibility of meeting the needs of thousands of refugees. With food and shelter secured, John, Nancy and their child now only needed to find gainful employment and prepare themselves for their first winter in Nova Scotia.

As it turned out, the Mosleys' first winter was an especially harsh one. Six inches of snow fell on the thirteenth of November and continued to accumulate on an almost daily basis. By Christmas day, temperatures had dropped low enough to freeze over the St. John River.

One Loyalist refugee who survived that winter later wrote,

> *"Many woman and children and some of the men, died from cold and exposure. Graves were dug with axes and shovels near the spot where our party had landed and there in stormy winter weather our loved ones were buried." A bachelor soldier recalled, "I daily see those, who have neither house nor home and scarcely nourishment, or Clothing to guard them against the Attacks of this rigorous season of the Year."*

As the winter months passed, the commissariat's initial provisions of flour, butter and pork ran out and potatoes soon became the staple of the Loyalist refugee diet in Parrtown. Conditions were so depressing that at least one white Loyalist was driven to take his own life. But John, Nancy and their child survived.

Fort Howe's victualling muster — the list of names of those who received food from the commissariat — recorded all three Mosley family members in its entries for May 1784. While the muster recorded John's name and his race, it only listed Nancy by her relationship (wife) and not by name. The list noted that her child was "under ten," but there is no reference to whether the child was a boy or girl.

With the approaching summer and its promise of fish, game and new crops, life could finally take a positive turn. John and Nancy Mosley had escaped the violence of slavery, the dangers of the revolution, the prospect of re-enslavement, a hazardous ship journey and their first winter in the northern colony. But within a month of their May appearance in the victualling muster, something upset the promise of a free and happier future.

Instead of recording three family members, the victualling muster for June of 1784 lists only John as a recipient of Fort Howe's provisions. Neither Nancy nor their child is on record as having received food. At some point between the two muster entries, the Mosleys had suffered some sort of marital breakdown. As we know that Nancy was alive until at least 1785, her absence in the muster records means that she had left John that summer, taking their child with her. Because the records after May 1784 make no reference to the youngest Mosley, in all likelihood their child died early that summer.

Marriages often do not survive the loss of a child, especially if the death is due to parental violence or a tragic accident. The stress of trying to establish a new life, once the distractions of war or personal threat are removed, can also be the undoing of a marriage. Whatever drove Nancy away from John that June is unknown — but there are tantalizing clues as to what may have happened, given the events of the fall of 1784.

Within three months of her last appearance alongside John Mosley's notation in Fort Howe's records, Nancy was once again living with her husband. This suggests two scenarios.

Nancy's temporary separation from John may have given her the time she need to regain some emotional stability, allowing her the breathing space to grieve and heal following the death of their only child. It may be that after regaining her perspective, she returned to John's home in the hopes of rebuilding their life.

It is also true that women who suffer abuse at the hands of their husbands often leave their attackers "for good" only to return at a later date, taken in by the man's promises of reform and rehabilitation. Nancy may have been an abused wife who left John at the end of May only to decide to give him another chance in September. Or it may simply have been an economic necessity on Nancy's part. Life in the wilderness demanded a greater mutual dependency on the part of married partners. The homemaker needed a provider for her survival and that of her children; the provider needed someone to prepare his meals and see to his home.

Whether it was a reunion based on forgiveness and reconciliation or one of necessity, by the September of 1784, Nancy and John Mosley were once again living under the same roof.

Violence erupted in the household. And on the twenty-seventh of September, Nancy lashed out. Picking up an ordinary dinner fork from the table, Nancy plunged it into John's temple, stabbing his head again and again. Nancy left John for dead and fled their cabin. It would be two days before John's friends realized they had not seen him or Nancy in the community. When Richard Corankapoon Wheeler, a fellow Black Loyalist, and his friends, John and Jane Walker, visited the Mosleys' cabin, they found John lying on the floor. The wounds that Nancy had inflicted with the iron table fork had proven fatal. John Mosley was dead.

Immediately, Walker and Wheeler sought out Daniel Keefe, one of Parrtown's constables, to report Mosley's death and accuse Nancy of his murder.

A week later, George Leonard, the Justice of the Peace, issued a warrant for Nancy's arrest. It also ordered Walker and Wheeler to appear in court on the date of Nancy's trial. Given that they had so quickly accused Nancy of killing her husband, the two Black Loyalists may have had prior knowledge of marital problems between the two. The heavy fines they would have to pay for failing to obey the judge's orders underscored the importance of their appearance in court.

Failure to "personally appear before the justices of

the Supreme Court" to "answer to such questions as the court might ask" would result in Wheeler being fined one hundred pounds (approximately $10,630 in current Canadian dollars) and Walker, fifty pounds. These penalties were to be levied on the two Black Loyalists' "respective goods and chattels, lands and tenements."

Parrtown's Justice of the Peace then called for a forensic examination of John Mosley's body. Determining the true cause of death would need the investigative skills of a doctor who had the expertise to perform an autopsy. That was Dr. Samuel Moore, who had earlier been made the coroner for the Loyalist settlement.

As the sheriff went to arrest Nancy, Moore finished his examination of John Mosley's body and submitted his report to a coroner's jury. The doctor wrote to the Justice of the Peace, reporting: "Agreeable to your request I examined the black man's head. I am perfectly satisfied he was murdered. After examining where the fork perforated the temporal bone of the skull, I sawed off the arch of the head and found the ventricles of the brain everywhere impacted with matter. The symptoms before death were also very obvious."

The coroner's jury concurred with Moore's analysis: "the fork was the occasion of his death." It is an indication of the strength of Nancy's rage that she was able to mortally wound John Mosley with just a table fork. Improbable as it may have seemed, the medical evidence was undeniable and the coroner's jury had no difficulty agreeing that a mere fork was the murder weapon.

It is interesting that historians writing in the nineteenth century found this so preposterous that when they wrote about John Mosley's murder they said he was "killed by a *pitchfork* in a domestic dispute." While these historians had their own interpretations of the murder weapon, they did not speculate on whether Nancy had initiated the fight that resulted in John Mosley's death, or whether she had used the fork in self-defense. That would fall to the grand jury to decide.

After Dr. Moore and the coroner's jury had rendered their judgment, the judge convened a grand jury of nineteen white men to decide if there was enough evidence to proceed with a murder trial. Despite the fact that Parrtown's Loyalists were on the wild fringes of the British Empire, they were careful to see that each step in Nancy's trial followed the legal procedures of the United Kingdom. The death of John Mosley, a Black Loyalist, was treated with the same care as the murder of a white Loyalist would have been.

It did not take the grand jury long to make its decision. It alleged that Nancy Mosley, with "malice aforethought, did make an assault and . . . with a certain iron fork of the value of sixpence, which . . . [she] held in her right hand, struck him, the said John Mozely, in and upon the head near unto the temple and that . . . [he] . . . did languish and of the mortal wound aforesaid on their oaths do say, that the said Nancy Mozely, him the said John Mozely, her said husband, in manner and by the means aforesaid, feloniously, traitorously, wilfully and of her malice aforethought, did kill and murder against the peace of our Lord and King, his Crown and dignity."

Not having heard any evidence other than the coroner's autopsy report, it might seem surprising that the grand jury believed that Nancy murdered John with "malice aforethought." It seems that, in the minds of the jury, the only guilty party in this violent domestic dispute was the wife. As was the law at the time, self-defense in the case of domestic abuse was not recognized as a legitimate legal defense.

In addition to these sexist attitudes, the period of Loyalist settlement was a racist era in which the courts regularly gave out much stiffer sentences to Africans than to whites who had committed the same offences. Race determined punishment. Given that Parrtown was known to hang its robbers, there was little hope for a Black woman convicted of murdering her husband.

For the next four months, Nancy's life was not her own. Not since her days as a slave had her movements been so curtailed, her social contacts so limited or her fate so uncertain as when she was imprisoned in Fort Howe's blockhouse, waiting for her trial to begin.

Although she had been arrested in October, Nancy did not appear in court until Thursday, February 3, 1785, to hear the charges against her. Her trial began on the third day of the very first session of New Brunswick's Supreme Court. The judge was Chief Justice George Duncan Ludlow, a Loyalist refugee from Long Island, New York, who had been one of that colony's Supreme Court judges.

Nancy was arraigned and tried the following day. Twelve white men sat in the jury; Chief Justice Ludlow presided. No defense lawyer is mentioned and it may be that Nancy was questioned directly by the chief justice. John Walker and Richard Corankapoon were called to provide testimony pertaining to the home life of the Black Loyalist couple, but if any other members of the Black community were in court, their presence is not mentioned in the official records.

The fact that Nancy's attack on her husband occurred during a domestic dispute indicated that it had been a crime of passion rather than a premeditated act. Nancy may not have intended to do more than simply inflict pain upon John Mosley, given that she assaulted him with a mere dinner fork. Whether the jury was asked to consider the state of Nancy's mental stability after the death of her only child just months before her husband's murder is not recorded — nor was there any consideration of the fact that Nancy might have suffered physical abuse at the hands of her husband prior to his murder.

Whatever mitigating circumstances may have been suggested to the jury, their verdict differed little from the grand jury's back in October. Although not charged with murdering John Mosley, Nancy was found guilty of manslaughter. While it was not as serious a crime as first-degree murder, it was still punishable by death. After hearing the jury's verdict, Nancy returned to prison where she had to wait until the following day to learn her sentence.

That she would be the first citizen of Parrtown to be hanged for murder seemed inevitable. On the day of Nancy's trial, two men of mixed race had been found guilty of burglary and were fully expected to face the gallows. However, one had been "recommended to mercy." On the day of his sentencing, the court was lenient and ordered his banishment from the colony. On the day following Nancy's trial, two white men were convicted of highway robbery and grand larceny. The courts condemned both of them to be hanged on Gallows Hill near Fort Howe. Once again, the court decided to show mercy to one man and reduced his sentence to banishment. If burglary, highway robbery and grand larceny were punished by hanging, there seemed to be no hope for a woman convicted of murdering her husband. However, the banishment of two guilty criminals also demonstrated that extenuating circumstances could persuade the courts to consider alternatives to execution.

Fortunately for her, Nancy's testimony touched a sympathetic chord in someone sitting in the courtroom. In that person's mind, Nancy was a woman who did not deserve to be hanged — and they knew of a loophole in English law that could save her life. While the name of Nancy's benefactor is not known, the legal loophole shared with her was one known to anyone familiar with English common law.

Perhaps a fellow Black Loyalist paid Nancy a visit in her prison cell where he told her about a trial in the thirteen colonies. He remembered how a crucial legal technicality had saved another's life and urged her to use it in Parrtown's court. Or her benefactor may have been a sympathetic white Loyalist who felt that Nancy deserved a second chance. Whoever her legal advisor was, Nancy returned to court on the fifth of February prepared to make a desperate attempt to escape the gallows.

When asked if she had anything to say before Chief Justice Ludlow handed down his sentence, Nancy made use of the advice she had received the day before and asked the court to grant her "the benefit of the clergy."

To the modern ear, this request might sound as if Nancy was simply asking for the counsel and prayers of a clergyman as she faced the prospect of her execution, but it was something far different. What Nancy asked for was the "benefit" that English common law gave to a clergyman who was charged with a serious offense. Rather than administering the established punishment for a crime, the British courts were more lenient if the convicted criminal was a cleric. Because of his special legal status, a clergyman was exempt from execution, torture or imprisonment. In effect, Nancy Mosley was asking that she be treated as a member of the clergy and receive the "benefit" English courts had granted since the Middle Ages.

While it was blatantly obvious that this Black Loyalist woman was neither a priest nor a pastor, another strange loophole in the English legal system said that a person's ability to read was sufficient evidence to have them recognized as a clergyman. Fortunately for Nancy, this exemption had been extended to both women and African slaves sixty years earlier. This second loophole said that anyone on trial for their first offense only had to read aloud a passage from the Bible to receive the benefit of the clergy.

Following the precedent of courts in both the former American colonies and Britain, Nancy only had to memorize a passage of scripture and recite it as she looked down on the Bible's pages. In the case of murder, rather than being hanged, a convicted clergyman's only punishment — or "benefit" — was an "M" branded on the base of his left thumb. The request for this special exemption was so common in the thirteen colonies that most courthouses had their own branding irons: "T" for thief and "M" for manslaughter.

When a judge granted the clergyman's benefit to a felon, the sheriff applied the hot iron to the criminal's thumb for about one second. The pain lasted for five minutes and the hand would be sore for at least seventy-two hours. The branding was done in open court before the judge, jury and those assembled. While humiliating and painful, it had the merit of not being fatal.

Chief Justice Ludlow considered Nancy Mosley's request. As an American Loyalist, he *could* continue to follow the practices and traditions that had been part of his legal training in New York. Alternately, he *could* decide that it would be a terrible miscarriage of justice to extend a clergyman's benefit to a convicted Black woman.

Ludlow decided that he would grant Nancy the benefit of clergy. Whether Nancy actually recited a portion of Psalms to secure this legal exemption goes unrecorded. (The practice of making the offender read from Scripture had been eliminated in the courts of Virginia in 1732 and this may have become the common practice in all the colonies by the time of the American Revolution.)

Instead of being hanged, Nancy Mosley was punished with the branding of her thumb in open court.

Forever marked with the letter "M" for the crime of manslaughter, Nancy was set free, her life spared. Whether she remained in Parrtown or moved to a Black Loyalist settlement within the colony goes unrecorded. Four years after Nancy's trial, the New Brunswick legislature ended the practice of branding thumbs, instead extending fines or a whipping to whoever received the benefit of clergy for any crime other than manslaughter.

Nancy might have vanished from the historical records except for the fact that just a month before she killed her husband the political boundaries had changed within the Maritime colonies. On August 16, 1784, the territory north of the Bay of Fundy was partitioned from Nova Scotia to become the colony of New Brunswick. As New Brunswick included Parrtown, Nancy Mosley's murder trial became historically significant for being the first of its kind in the new colony. One hundred years after Nancy was sentenced, the historian Joseph Lawrence described the Mosley murder in these words: "The incident is entitled to a place in New Brunswick history, the more so, as Mosley was one of the grantees of Parr Town and as such in the Revolution was loyal to his Sovereign." It is significant that John's wartime service was remembered, a rare citation for any Black Loyalist who settled in New Brunswick. Typical of the Victorian era's historians, however, is the failure to recognize the service of a Black Loyalist woman.

The scandal of her husband's murder blotted out Nancy Mosley's role as a supporter of the British Crown during the American Revolution. Today, we remember her only as a convicted murderer. However, Nancy *did* receive mercy within a judicial system that did not favour women or Blacks. Her treatment is a rare exception in the ongoing history of Black Loyalists and the New Brunswick courts.

CHAPTER 6
Edward Burr: Fiddler and Gravedigger

Edward Burr was a Black Loyalist who, despite the racism of his day, found a crucial niche for himself in Saint John society during the first half of the nineteenth century. He is remarkable for being one of only eighteen people of African descent in New Brunswick who, in the first fifty years of the colony, had amassed enough property and possessions to warrant writing a will. Burr's life is an exceptional one in the annals of New Brunswick's Black Loyalist past. Undeterred by the racist obstacles in his path, he found a place within white society and experienced a prosperity known to very few of his Black contemporaries.

There is nothing in Edward Burr's first years in New Brunswick that would have predicted his being anything more than a common labourer in the Loyalist colony. At thirty-three, Burr had come to the colony with his wife,

Amy, and three children under the age of ten. There is no documentary evidence for the name of his evacuation ship or the details of his earlier life as a slave in the United States. Burr's name first appears in historical records on a 1784 list of the hundreds of white and Black Loyalists who received rations from Fort Howe's commissariat.

Perched high above the harbour, the garrison at Fort Howe had guarded the mouth of the St. John River against rebel attacks for the past six years. Now, instead of watching for invading privateers, the fort's personnel served the Crown by keeping order in the rapidly expanding Loyalist settlement. Fort Howe's commissary was now the distribution centre for the food and provisions provided by the British government. It was responsible for "victualling" a staggering total of 12,000 Loyalist refugees during their first year in New Brunswick.

Not everyone in Saint John received provisions from Fort Howe. Only those who were considered to be true Loyalists could expect to be given regular supplies of food. In the language of the era, these were people who "from an attachment to His Majesty's Government had abandoned the United States and decided to continue [with] his subjects in this Province." The Crown was only obligated to distribute provisions to free Blacks since they, like whites, had become refugees because of their loyalty to the Crown. However, an enslaved Black only received provisions as a member of a white Loyalist's household. The slave was given food as portioned out by the master. Edward Burr's inclusion in Fort Howe's victualling list indicates that he was recognized as both a free man and as a loyal supporter of King George III.

From the outset of Loyalist settlement, the free provision

of food supplied by Fort Howe was only intended to be a temporary measure to support the Loyalists in their first year of settlement. The refugees of the American Revolution were expected to be establishing themselves on farms or in trades as they were receiving government assistance.

When loyal refugees arrived in what became New Brunswick, most remained in Parrtown and Carleton, settling on town lots that they received through a land draw in 1783. Other Loyalists immediately went up the St. John River to settle in Kingston, Maugerville and St. Anne's Point (Fredericton). It would not be until 1784 that land along the river was surveyed and distributed. Those who had received town lots in what is now Saint John had been given enough land to build a house on, but it was not enough land to grow crops. To receive land in the interior that was suitable for farming, Loyalists in "town" wrote petitions to the colony's government.

In the spring of 1785, Edward Burr decided that his best opportunity for a new life would be joining with twelve other Black Loyalists who were petitioning the New Brunswick government for land grants. These men hoped to obtain farmland along the east side of Belleisle Bay near the white Loyalist settlement of Kingston, about fifty kilometres up the river from Saint John.

However, Burr's first attempt to become a farmer on his own land was unsuccessful. For reasons not recorded in the documents of the era, the Black Loyalist settlement at Belleisle Bay either was never established or was abandoned within a few months' time. Despite this setback, some of the Black Loyalists liked what they saw in the region. Two of the men whose names were on the Belleisle petition settled at Milkish on the lower part of the Kingston Peninsula at a later date. Edward Burr decided to remain on the St. John River, settling further up the river from Belleisle in Grimross (Gagetown).

Eight years after his failed attempt to help found a Black settlement, Burr's name appeared in the christening rolls of Grimross's Anglican congregation. While the records do not indicate Burr's occupation at the time, they do indicate that he was the father of Rose Ann Burr.

Baptism in the Anglican Church had a special significance for Black Loyalists: According to the church's theology, baptized persons were "all one and equal in Christ." Here, they were equal with white believers. Black Loyalist Samuel Burke is another example of someone who, while seeking financial compensation from the British government for his wartime service, cited his christening as evidence that he was, indeed, a free man. William Holchapan, who came to New Brunswick on the *Amity's Production* in June of 1783 had it noted in the *Book of Negroes* that he was "born free and baptised [in England] in the year 1779."

Rose Ann Burr's baptism in Gagetown on November 14, 1793, may have been her parents' attempt to give their daughter a greater standing in New Brunswick society. Given that some Loyalists still had enslaved Africans as part of their "property," the colony's white settlers did not view free Black Loyalists as their equals. For Edward Burr and his wife, becoming Anglicans — rather than joining one of the all-Black Baptist congregations along the St. John River — had the potential of giving the family greater opportunities within colonial society.

Being part of the denomination that was New Brunswick's established church could improve a Black Loyalist's chances of acceptance and employment. But even within the Anglican communion, Blacks were not treated as fellow congregants. Typically, they sat in pews at the back of churches alongside the slaves of white parishioners.

Rose Ann Burr's christening occurred two years after 222 of New Brunswick's Black Loyalists left the colony for Sierra Leone in 1791. Frustrated with being treated as second-class citizens, a large portion of the colony's Black Loyalists crossed the Atlantic to found a settlement in West Africa that promised them land, equality and self rule. It was a tremendous opportunity for a second chance at prosperity. Despite its promise of a better future, the Burr family decided not to join an exodus that included many people they had come to know during their first ten years in New Brunswick. The reasons for that decision are lost to history.

Having reached the age of forty-four, Edward Burr had already missed out on two opportunities to further his family's prosperity. He had not been able to establish a farming community with fellow Black Loyalists and he had not emigrated to Sierra Leone. After almost a decade of living along the St. John River, Burr pulled up stakes and took his family downriver to Saint John to seek his fortune. Back in the community where he and Amy had begun life as refugees, Burr finally found his path to prosperity as the city's gravedigger.

Although it was certainly unconventional, Edward Burr's career choice enabled him to provide for his wife and daughters. Among the Black Loyalists who were making comfortable livings for themselves by the 1790s were mariners, streetcar drivers, grocers, blacksmiths, valets and merchants. Burr's inclusion in the city's middle class was based on his proficiency with both the shovel and the fiddle. By day, he dug graves in the city's burial ground; by night, he provided music for dancing parties.

Gravedigging, a job that few people would be willing to pursue, turned out to be a profitable occupation for Burr. Traditionally, gravediggers were on the fringes of polite society. They provided a necessary but unpopular service. It is likely that no white Saint Johner would even consider taking the position. In this case, the same racist system that marginalized its Black citizens gave Edward Burr the opportunity for steady employment and a decent living.

Typically in this era, people were buried in graveyards of the churches they had attended in life. The man responsible for seeing to the interment of the dead for each congregation was known as a sexton. Early nineteenth-century cities would have a number of churches and therefore a number of sextons.

However, in the case of Saint John, churches had not yet been built. Without churches, there was nowhere to bury their dead. The city needed a community cemetery and a gravedigger. What became known as "the Old Burial Ground," located between Sydney and Carmarthen Streets, received its first body in 1784. The oldest surviving tombstone bears a death date of July 13, 1784.

When the Burr family returned to Saint John sometime after Rose Ann's christening in 1793, almost a decade had passed since the establishment of the burial ground. The names and terms of the city's previous gravediggers are unknown, but once Edward Burr was hired for the job, he would be Saint John's gravedigger for almost forty years. A nineteenth-century historian has estimated that the graveyard held as many as 12,000 burials sites. Burr would have dug a significant number of them.

No records survive to indicate what Burr was paid, but given that he died with enough property to bequeath to his heirs, his unpopular work, combined with his earnings from fiddle playing, provided enough to pay for more than life's bare necessities. Those earnings made Burr a part of Saint John's very small Black middle class.

Given that Saint John's 1785 charter of incorporation forbid Blacks from living and working within the city, it is especially remarkable that Burr was able to become its gravedigger. The charter did permit the mayor "from time to time as he shall think proper" to "license any of the said people of colour to reside in the said city and to carry on any business or occupation which he shall think fit." The role of the gravedigger was of such importance that the mayor made an exception on Burr's behalf, allowing him to work and live within Saint John.

Despite the severe restrictions placed on Black Loyalists in Saint John's city charter, there were over a dozen other men and women who were able to acquire "the means of getting and having a comfortable support for themselves and their families." In addition to four Black men who settled in York County, fourteen people of African descent living in Saint John managed to overcome the odds stacked against them in racist New Brunswick. When they died, they were able to leave property and possessions to friends and family.

Caesar Closs came to Saint John on the *Duchess of Gordon* in June of 1783. Two years earlier, he had been enslaved by Bowes Reed, a prominent Patriot in Burlington, New Jersey. As is too often the case with stories of Black Loyalists, primary sources are devoid of any mention of the next fourteen years of Closs's life. However, on February 28, 1797, "the kindred and creditors of the deceased" were summoned to appear in court to discuss the administration of Closs's "estate." The Black Loyalist was described as a "labourer."

Although his particular trade is not mentioned, Closs had been, in the words of Saint John's charter of incorporation, "good, discreet and honest" enough to receive a license from the mayor. Within just fourteen years of his arrival in Saint John, the former slave had worked hard enough to acquire an "estate" and became the first Black Loyalist mentioned in New Brunswick's probate records.

Seven years later, when Gabriel Johnson died without a will, the administration of his estate was granted to a fellow Black Loyalist named Robert Johnston. During the American Revolution, Gabriel had escaped from slavery in Quibbletown, New Jersey, and served with the British troops for the remainder of the war. After arriving in Saint John, Gabriel became a mariner — an important job in a city that would increasingly rely on shipping as the engine of its economy.

A greater glimpse into the life of this Black Loyalist mariner is found in the will of his widow, Sylvia Johnson. Unlike her husband, Sylvia composed a will, naming property and heirs. The Johnson home was on St. James Street, a street in the south end of Saint John. Two other Black Loyalist families found in New Brunswick's probate records lived on this street as well. This may have been the beginning of a neighbourhood of middle-class Black Loyalists who had received licenses from the mayor to live and work within Saint John.

Having no children of her own, Sylvia Johnson willed her home to her goddaughter, Sylvia Bryant, a "black woman of City of Saint John." The remainder of the Johnson estate went to Robert Jenkins who was described as being a "black man" and a carpenter. Sylvia also bequeathed her household furniture and clothing to Robert's wife, Hannah Jenkins. Interestingly, the only two witnesses to her will were women: Ann and Mary Sharman.

Though the will omits details that would interest future historians, Sylvia Johnson's last testament hints at the many strands that bound the early Black Loyalist community together. There was a common faith (she had been named the godmother of Sylvia Bryant at her christening), common ties outside of her husband's work (the friendship with the Jenkins family) and a geographical proximity to other Blacks within Saint John. And in Sylvia Johnson's case, there was value placed on other women as witnesses and heirs.

William Holmes came to Saint John with his wife and son in 1783. Twenty-two years later, the *Saint John Gazette* noted that Holmes, a "black man of this city," would have his estate administered by Joseph Nutting. William Junior received "his birthright, house and lot 494." The residue of Holmes's estate went to his daughters, Jane and Elizabeth. Since Joseph Nutting was a driver of a horse-drawn carriage by trade, it may be that this had also been Holmes's occupation within Saint John.

William Holmes Junior died half a dozen years later. While he did not make out a will, those listed as his "fellow bondsmen" were Peter Thompson and Lawrence Broughton, "black men, all of Saint John." Again, there are hints here of connections within the small middle-class component of the city's Black Loyalists. Within the next twenty years, both Thompson and Broughton would have their estates distributed to heirs through Saint John's probate court.

Peter Thompson died without a will near the end of

1818. His widow, Phillis Thompson (described as being "of colour") administered the estate, which was valued at £725 (approximately $77,075 in current Canadian dollars). Described as a "labourer," Thompson had two grocers, a blacksmith, a yeoman and two merchants as participants in the distribution of his estate, which suggests that his occupation would have put him within a similar stratum of society.

When a Black Loyalist mariner named Henry Richards died, the probate court granted the administration of his estate to his widow, Sarah Richards, on February 10, 1820. His fellow bondsmen were listed as Lawrence Broughton (already noted in William Holmes Junior's will) and Johmall Cole, "men of colour, all of the City of Saint John."

Samuel Quarry, "a man of colour," must have had a sense that his end was near. He had his will drawn up on May 9, 1821, and was dead within two months. His wife, Mary, was the sole executrix and inherited this "labourer's" entire estate.

The next Black Loyalist's will that is on file with the probate court is that of Susan Murdock, the "widow of John Murdock, coloured man." She, too, died shortly after writing her will in October of 1825. The family home on lot 721 in Queen's Ward was to be "held by [the] executor" for Susan's son Robert Fletcher "in such a manner as he cannot sell the same." If Robert did not wish to live in the house, then it was to be rented "for his benefit as long as he lives." A Black woman lived in a house on the back of lot 721 and Susan's will decreed that she was to "continue there until her death."

Murdock's will suggests a resolve to retain the home acquired by hard work in a city that did not welcome Black Loyalist occupants. She may have feared that her son would sell the family property for quick cash rather than recognizing the value that land would have in a growing city. The will also shows that Black Loyalists acted as landlords to others in their community and that those less fortunate were treated with consideration.

Although John Stevens died on February 10, 1829, his estate's administration was not granted to anyone until ten months later. A widower, Stevens had no heirs to whom his estate could be bequeathed. The four men mentioned in Stevens's probate record were white merchants of Saint John. Since these men had loaned the Black Loyalist money for "his support" and had covered "his and his wife's funeral expenses," they asked to be the benefactors of Stevens's estate. What this record reveals is that a Black Loyalist in Saint John was prosperous enough that four white businessmen were willing to loan him money and were confident that they would be repaid.

Lawrence Broughton, whose name appeared in the probate records of two other Black Loyalists, died on December 29, 1827, at the age of sixty-eight. The probate court granted the administration of his property and possessions to his widow, Susannah Broughton, in July of the following year. When an inventory was taken of Broughton's worldly possessions, his half lot on St. James Street was valued at fifty pounds (approximately $5,315 in current Canadian dollars).

Broughton had come to Saint John with his wife when he was only twenty-four years old. At some point, he became the "confidential servant" to William Pagan, one of the city's most prominent businessmen and politicians. Pagan was a merchant, a shipbuilder, a staunch member of the Church of Scotland — and a bachelor. With no wife to run his household, care for his grooming or welcome guests into his brick home on Germain Street, Pagan needed a valet or butler to manage his domestic affairs. Lawrence Broughton served Pagan right up until the latter's death in Fredericton where Pagan had been attending the colony's legislative council. The Black Loyalist was sixty years old at the time of his employer's death.

Broughton must have been well regarded by those who were part of Pagan's business and political circles. Even though it occurred eight years after his employer's death, Broughton's own demise was considered important enough to be reported in the *New Brunswick Courier*. Before the Black Loyalist's passing, only five death notices for those of African descent appeared in the colony's press between 1786 and 1827. Typically, the notice was extremely brief — as in this 1818 line of type: "d. Yesterday, Peter Thomson, man of color, age 60."

John Ming left his entire estate to his wife, Hannah, when he died in 1832. While his will fails to give his profession, it is nevertheless interesting for its mention of his executor, "friend John Lewis, a coloured man." Described in the same manner, Lewis's name would appear in the 1835 will of the Black Loyalist Robert Campbell who worked in Saint John as a "hand cartman" — either a peddler or a baggage carrier. Middle-class Blacks knew one another and relied on each other in both life and death.

Robert Campbell's will bequeathed his home on lot 760 and the property on a second Saint John lot to his wife, Mary, who was to continue to lease the lots to Rolla Campbell and Amy Campbell "during their natural lives." The hand cartman had done well enough in his work to acquire property and to earn an income from it as a landlord.

Only four of New Brunswick's early probate records have to do with Blacks who lived outside of Saint John. Charles King, a "yeoman" in York County's parish of Kingsclear, willed his entire estate to his wife, Hannah, upon his death in 1821. Anthony Warren, presumably a farmer, had appointed another man in Kingsclear to be his administrator upon his death in 1822. In that same year, Edward Peters, "a man of colour," died, having appointed his wife, Ann, as his executor.

Situated just above Fredericton, Kingsclear was the site of a Black Loyalist settlement that also included Black refugees from the War of 1812. It is hard to know with absolute certainty whether King, Warren and Peters were refugees of the American Revolution or the War of 1812.

The same can be said for William Belile in the parish of Douglas. His death in 1835 puts him late enough in New Brunswick's history to have been either a Black Loyalist or a Black Refugee. (An elector in Fredericton in 1812 had the same name and if this is the man under consideration, then he was definitely a Black Loyalist.) Regardless, his will demonstrates that a man of African descent could, at times, beat the odds and prosper in a racist society.

Belile's estate, which was valued at one hundred pounds (approximately $10,630 in current Canadian dollars), was bequeathed to his two stepdaughters, Abigail and Rose Burt. One of the witnesses of his will was Henry George Clopper, the president of Fredericton's first bank. One of the estate appraisers was a tax collector named George Sloot. The Black farmer had important connections to the middle and upper echelons of New Brunswick society.

New Brunswick's early probate records seem an unlikely source for revealing the story of the Black Loyalists, but the sum of their sparse details paints a picture in large strokes. Despite the restrictions on employment and residency within Saint John, Black Loyalists were able to make valuable contributions to the economy of the city through a variety of trades within the middle class: driving carriages, sailing ships, transporting goods, providing skilled labour, managing households, building and renting houses and selling groceries. Many of these trades would have been acquired during the Black Loyalists' time as slaves or during their service to the British Crown in the American Revolution.

The probate records also show the close ties that maintained the members of Saint John's Black Loyalist community. Common names appear in several wills, demonstrating a reliance on one another. Even the mention of a godchild gives evidence that a common faith united many Black Loyalists. Two of those leaving estates to heirs lived on the same street as Edward Burr, the city's gravedigger.

Although white Loyalists appreciated the part that Edward Burr played in the burial of their friends and family members, they did not permit Blacks to be interred in the city's graveyard. Compiled in 1903, a 903-page report on the epitaphs found in Saint John's Old Burying Ground failed to list anyone who was known to be a Black Loyalists — not even Edward Burr, the cemetery's long-serving gravedigger. Granted, those who made up the working class of the city — Black or white — would only be able to afford a wooden marker over their graves and those would inevitably disappear over time. However, there were middle-class Blacks in the city between 1784 and 1835 who could have afforded an engraved headstone as readily as their white counterparts. But no such tombstones existed in Saint John. The city's racist policies even extended to where a person was laid to rest.

If Edward Burr dug graves for his fellow Blacks, they would have been in graveyards apart from those of white settlers.

Blacks were sometimes buried at the far edges of church graveyards, segregated in death as they had been in life. The earliest example of a New Brunswick cemetery that allowed for the burial of both white and Black Loyalists would not be established until almost ten years after Edward Burr's death. St. Peter's Anglican Church in Kingsclear, just outside of Fredericton, and All Saints' Anglican Church in St. Andrew's both had fully integrated graveyards. These would not be duplicated elsewhere in the colony for decades.

Although being both Black and a gravedigger might have distanced Burr from Saint John's white society, he was, nevertheless, much sought after as an entertainer. Widely known as "Old Ned," his talents as a fiddler made him the nineteenth century equivalent of a DJ — an essential part of any lively social gathering.

The will that Burr drew up two months before his demise in 1834 reveals the degree of prosperity this Black Loyalist had achieved in his twin careers as a gravedigger and a musician. To his wife, Amy, Burr bequeathed the western half of his lot of land on St. James Street as well as two thirds of his furniture and personal property. Burr's two daughters, Rosanna and Margaret, were given the eastern half of his city lot (just south of Queen Square) and one third of his personal property.

While the wills of other middle-class Black Loyalists generally named witnesses and executors from within the Black community, Burr's will is interesting for having white Loyalists as his witnesses and executors. Furthermore, these white friends were all men of note. Thomas Sandall was a merchant who traded in the West Indies, his son John Sandall had a ship brokerage business and Daniel Ansley would later become an alderman and Justice of the Peace.

How Edward Burr came to know these men and include them in the dispersal of his worldly goods is just one of the hundreds of lost stories of the Black Loyalists.

When he died at the age of eighty-four on April 28, 1834, Burr was considered newsworthy enough to have a notice of his passing published in the city's newspaper. A later historian summed up the Black Loyalist's life, noting, "The first grave-digger was a colored man named Edward Burr, who for fifty years served in that capacity. Burr was a character in his way and well known. His sombre occupation of the day was relieved at night by his playing the fiddle for dancing parties."

Coming to New Brunswick as a penniless refugee, Edward Burr found his niche in white Loyalist society by providing two very different services for the people of Saint John. As a gravedigger and a fiddle player, he eventually joined the middle class and acquired a house in the city's south end. A valued member of his community, Edward Burr is a rare example of a Black Loyalist who was able to realize the potential of the freedom he had earned in the midst of the American Revolution.

PART TWO:
Second Exodus

CHAPTER 7
Thomas Peters: A Passion for Justice

Ordinary fellow.

That's how Thomas Peters was described in November of 1783.

The officials who recorded the names of Black Loyalists leaving New York City had to give physical descriptions of the refugees as well as their ages and the year they sided with the British forces. The forty-five-year-old sergeant may not have made a great first impression on that November day, but in the years that followed, Peters would go on to prove that he was anything but an ordinary fellow.

Slave traders captured Peters in what is now Nigeria when he was twenty-two years old and shipped him off to Louisiana. After becoming the property of William Campbell in Wilmington, North Carolina, Peters met another enslaved African named Murphy Steele. The two men escaped their masters in 1776 and found sanctuary within the British lines. Now recognized by the British government as free men, Peters and Steele enlisted in the Black Pioneers.

This all-Black corps had been organized by General Henry Clinton, the commander-in-chief of British forces in North America from 1778 to 1782, just prior to Sir Guy Carleton. In the military jargon of the eighteenth century, a "pioneer" was a soldier who cleared land, dug latrines and completed other engineering duties. He did not take up arms and fight. When the British recruited Black Loyalists such as Peters and Steele, they allowed them to serve as pioneers rather than as regular soldiers.

Free Blacks could be non-commissioned (lower ranking) officers, but the commissioned officers were always white. Despite these limitations, the Black Pioneers were adequately clothed and fed and treated with respect. Their numbers never grew to more than sixty; new recruits were barely able to replace those who died from smallpox and fatigue.

Despite having a non-combative role, Thomas Peters was wounded twice during the course of the American Revolution, so his duties must have taken him close to battles on a number of occasions. Both Peters and his friend Steele served in Rhode Island, New York, Philadelphia, South Carolina and, finally, in New York City. During the course of the war, both men were promoted to the rank of sergeant, which put them each in charge of a squad of a dozen men. The Black Pioneers were the last unit of Loyalist soldiers to leave Manhattan in November of 1783, serving their distant king to the very end of the revolution.

Having enjoyed the company of free Blacks throughout the revolution, members of the Black Pioneers remained together as they sought refuge in Nova Scotia at the war's end. Although they were formally disbanded at the end of the revolution, the veterans boarded evacuation vessels in "companies" under the leadership of their former officer.

Peter's friend Murphy Steele was among the Black Pioneer veterans who boarded the evacuation vessel *Joseph* that was bound for Annapolis Royal in November of 1783. Like Peters, Steele had also been described as an "ordinary fellow" when his name was entered into the *Book of Negroes*. Despite the fact that names were often misspelled in the ledger and physical descriptions were uncomplimentary, it would become a valuable source of information about the Black Loyalists who eventually made their homes in Nova Scotia, New Brunswick and other parts of the British Empire. Had the British official who filled out the columns in the *Book of Negroes* taken the time to ask Steele about his wartime experience, he would have discovered how inappropriate it was to have described the sergeant as "ordinary."

Two years earlier, Steele had a vision that was so astounding that its message was recorded in a letter to Sir Henry Clinton. In early August of 1781, Steele was in the barracks on New York's Water Street. Since it was noontime, when Steele heard a man's voice call him by name, he knew that he was not having a dream.

The voice told him that General Washington "must surrender himself and his troops to the king's army and that if he did not, the wrath of God would fall upon them." It went on to say that if Washington failed to surrender, then Clinton should raise "all the blacks in America to fight against him." Steele ignored the voice, but it repeated its message to him several times over the next few days.

Finally on the thirteenth of August, the voice insisted

that Steele convey the message to Sir Henry Clinton, the British commander-in-chief. Steele refused, saying that since he could not see the person speaking, he was afraid to go to Clinton.

The voice finally revealed itself as being that of God and again insisted that Steele convey the message to Clinton. If Washington did not surrender, Steele was warned, then Clinton and Cornwallis were "to put an end to this rebellion for . . . the Lord would be on their side."

In the end, Steele went to Clinton. The Black Loyalist's vision became the subject of a letter that has survived to this day, but the commander-in-chief did not act on what Steele claimed to have heard. If the voice was nothing more than the product of an overactive imagination on the part of Murphy Steele, it nevertheless reveals that the Black Loyalist believed that "all the Blacks in America" could defeat Washington and that God was on their side. An odd little sidebar in the story of the Black Pioneers, it reveals the faith that free Black men had in the justice inherent in their struggle.

Neither Steele nor Peters left New York City as bachelors. Peters married a single mother named Sally after she escaped her master in South Carolina in 1779. In addition to twelve-year-old Clara, the Black Loyalist couple brought their eighteenth-month-old son, John, with them when they boarded the *Joseph*. Steele's wife was Mary, who had escaped slavery in Virginia when she was just nineteen.

Carrying sixty-five Black passengers, the *Joseph* left New York City on November 9, 1783, and set sail for Annapolis Royal on the western coast of Nova Scotia. It was supposed to be no more than a two-week journey, but just as the ship reached the Bay of Fundy a tropical hurricane struck the region, driving the Peters's evacuation ship off course and damaging its masts and sails. Incapable of continuing to Nova Scotia, the *Joseph* took refuge in Bermuda.

The Black Loyalist passengers spent the winter on the island while they waited for the *Joseph* to be repaired. It would not be until May of 1784 that Thomas Peters, Murphy Steele and their fellow evacuees would finally step foot on the shores of Annapolis Royal. The disembarking passengers had endured slavery in the United States, risked their lives in the American Revolution and had now survived a long and dangerous voyage to Nova Scotia.

Although two thirds of the *Joseph*'s refugees had not been members of the Black Pioneers, they had spent the last six months looking to Peters and Steele, who were the highest-ranking officers present. The two sergeants' experiences as trusted leaders during the war and during their time in Bermuda would turn out to be invaluable training for the new challenges they would face in defending the rights of Black Loyalists in Nova Scotia and New Brunswick.

White Loyalists quickly recognized Peters's leadership skills and put him in charge of the Blacks who had settled around the Annapolis Basin. The families of sixty-five Black Pioneer veterans settled in Brindley Town just outside of Digby. For a time, it would be the second largest settlement of free Blacks in Nova Scotia.

It quickly became apparent, as land was allocated to the Loyalists over the next three months, that the white refugees were receiving larger and better lots than their Black counterparts. At the same time, the Nova Scotia government promised three years' worth of provisions to white refugees, but Black Loyalists received only eighty days' worth of free provisions. (The distribution of supplies to Black Loyalists differed from one British garrison's commissary to another. Across the Bay of Fundy in Parrtown, Black Loyalists received provisions on the same basis as their white counterparts.) After that time, the free Blacks would have to work on road building projects if they wanted further assistance.

Incensed by this treatment, Peters and Steele petitioned John Parr, Nova Scotia's governor, within three months of their arrival in Annapolis County. Parr acquiesced to their demands, giving them one-acre town lots within Brindley Town and farm lots nearby. However, when the Black Loyalists tried to settle on their farm lots they were twice forced to relocate when whites claimed that the land was theirs.

Despite having insufficient land and government provisions, the Black Loyalists fed themselves with fish from the Bay of Fundy and produce from small kitchen gardens. They formed Anglican and Methodist congregations and received financing for a school, but, until the land issue was resolved, the Black Loyalist community would not be able to sustain itself for very long.

Tired of government inaction, Thomas Peters and the families of at least fifteen Black Pioneer veterans left the Annapolis Basin. They crossed the Bay of Fundy in July of 1785 to seek their fortune in the newly created colony of New Brunswick. (Murphy Steele, it seems, remained behind in Nova Scotia.)

Less than three months after his arrival, Peters sought justice for his people, petitioning Lieutenant-Governor Carleton for farmland along the St. John River. In the end, some families were given town lots — but with as much as thirty kilometres between their town lots and the farm land they had been granted, this was hardly the solution Thomas Peters had hoped for.

Over the next five years, the determined Black Pioneer sergeant filed five more petitions for land with the New Brunswick government, only to have each one denied.

In 1790, petitioners styling themselves as "the Free Blacks of the Province of New Brunswick," made Thomas Peters their attorney. They had recently learned that a charitable society in England was prepared to build and support a school back in Brindley Town and they wanted the same opportunity in New Brunswick. To accomplish this, they gave Thomas Peters the power to negotiate with the colonial government on their behalf, being "sensible that it would be to Our Advantage if our Affairs were to be transacted by One Person Nominated and Appointed to Act for and in behalf of the whole of us; in all matters both Civil and Religious."

While this petition also fell on deaf ears, it proved to be the next step in Thomas Peters's rise to leadership among New Brunswick's Black Loyalists. Within a few months of the failed school petition, Peters was once again chosen to represent Black Loyalists. However, in this case, the fifty-two-year-old veteran would not be making an appeal to a small colonial government; he would be going to London, England, to seek justice from the British government itself.

CHAPTER 8
Thomas Peters: A New Promised Land

Sailing to Nova Scotia from the United States in 1783 had failed to fulfil the dream of freedom. Sailing to New Brunswick from Annapolis Royal in 1785 did not result in equality. But perhaps sailing from New Brunswick to the very heart of the British Empire in 1790 would turn the tide of Black Loyalist fortunes.

As the designated leader for the Black Loyalists, Thomas Peters spoke on behalf of "102 people at Annapolis who have deputed your memorialist to represent their unhappy situation" as well as "about 100 families or more at New Brunswick in like unprovided and destitute condition." Seeing Peters as their best hope for justice, Black Loyalists trusted him to act on their behalf "in all matters both civil and religious."

In travelling to London, Thomas Peters became the forerunner of civil rights activists in North America. No Black man had ever represented so many of his people in seeking justice from one of the world's most powerful empires.

Unlike the majority of leaders within the Black Loyalist communities of Nova Scotia, Peters was not a clergyman. His experiences in achieving his goals had come from years of military life during the revolution and his persistent writing of petitions to colonial governments. Unlike the Black clergy, Peters represented people scattered over a wide geographical area rather than those living in concentrated Black Loyalist settlements or those who were members of Black congregations within white settlements. In short, Thomas Peters was the first political leader of New Brunswick's Black Loyalists, a man whom they had chosen as their envoy to the British government.

As well as recounting the injustices that Black Loyalists had suffered in seeking land, Peters also outlined how they had been denied fundamental rights such as access to courts, trial by jury and the right to vote. He wanted to "procure for himself and his fellow-sufferers some establishment where they may attain a competent settlement for themselves and be enabled by their industrious exertions to become useful subjects to his Majesty." The Black Pioneers veteran sought nothing less than his people's equality within the British Empire. It was a lofty goal for a man once described as being "an ordinary fellow."

By November of 1790, Peters had made his way to the capital of the British Empire. After meeting the abolitionist Granville Sharp, Peters was introduced to Henry Dundas, the secretary of state for the Home Department. Dundas immediately recognized what the governments of Nova Scotia and New Brunswick had failed (or refused) to see — the unfair treatment of a people who had served the Crown during wartime.

Dundas lost no time in sending off orders to the two colonial governments instructing them to immediately grant the land the Black Loyalists had been promised and to "make them some atonement for the injury they have suffered by [Nova Scotia's and New Brunswick's] unaccountable delay and I must desire to receive from you, as soon as possible, a particular account from you of your proceeding in consequence."

Dundas's instructions to the two colonial governors did more than direct them to grant fair — and long overdue — land allotments to the Black Loyalists. It also informed John Parr and Thomas Carleton that the British government was prepared to provide transportation for Thomas Peters, his family "and such other Blacks as may be disposed to become settlers at Sierra Leone."

While Peters was in London, British abolitionists had offered the Black Loyalist an unanticipated opportunity: the chance to found a colony in West Africa that would be settled and governed by emancipated Blacks. Even more amazing, Dundas intended to underwrite this exodus and all of its attendant expenses with government funds.

Far from being nuisances on the fringes of Nova Scotia's and New Brunswick's white society, the Black Loyalists had captured the attention and compassion of a British cabinet minister. Although neither colonial governor was dismissed nor reprimanded, it was clear that their political superiors in London were not pleased with how Parr and Carleton had treated the Black Loyalists.

As the colonial governments recovered from the sting of Dundas's correspondence in the fall of 1791, Thomas Peters returned to New Brunswick. Just days after Peters arrived home, John Clarkson arrived in Halifax. As the agent of the Sierra Leone Company, Clarkson would see to it that the colonial governments followed through on Dundas's instructions. The Englishman recruited Black Loyalists in Nova Scotia to colonize Sierra Leone while Peters was responsible for spreading the news of the West African colony to those awaiting his return in New Brunswick.

Writing to Clarkson from Saint John in early October, Peters said, "This is to inform you of my arrival in this place and find the people in high spirits — regarding the proposals, I mean as soon as I can to proceed to Frederictown and return with all speed back to this place and from this to Annapolis."

Over the next two months, Peters travelled up and down the St. John River, visiting Black Loyalist settlements and speaking to those who laboured in the colony's larger towns. He also recruited the free Blacks who still lived in Digby, Brindley Town and Annapolis Royal. Considering Black Loyalists had been treated as unwanted neighbours in New Brunswick since its founding, Peters was surprised to discover how opposed some of its white citizens were to the Sierra Leone venture.

Based on testimony from Thomas Peters, John Clarkson later summarized white opposition in his journal.

> *From his account the people at New Brunswick are in a deplorable state, the Agent appointed for carrying on the business (who is Secretary to the Governor) has done everything in his power to prevent their going by telling them that I intended to sell them for the Company and that Peters was to have so much per head for his trouble.*
>
> *They have also been guilty of forgery, in producing indentures and agreements on the part of the Blacks to work upon their lands and in their*

> *service for certain terms, at the same time have said that if they should offer to go, they would prosecute them for not performing their contract and others to prevent some of them from going would not pay them their just debts, telling them that if they would stay they should have their money, but if they were determined to go they would not pay them one farthing and some of them actually came down to Halifax without receiving that which [they] probably have been working for many months to obtain.*
>
> *What a pity I could not visit Saint John to make these wretches act like men! I think I have reason to say it would have been the case here [Halifax], had I not arrived just as I did.*

By the time all of the settler recruits arrived in Halifax, there were 1,190 men, women and children ready to leave the Maritimes for Africa. Peters had recruited 222 of them in New Brunswick — seventy-two men, sixty-four women and eighty-six children.

The ships carrying New Brunswick's Black Loyalists arrived in Halifax on the twenty-seventh of November. Peters immediately threw himself into working with John Clarkson to prepare the excited emigrants for their journey to Sierra Leone. Along with two Nova Scotia clergymen, Peters was put in charge of hearing the passengers' concerns and complaints. One bit of correspondence between Peters and Clarkson illustrates the Black Loyalist's role as a mediator and spokesman.

"As it is the last Christmas Day we shall ever see in America, that it may please your Honour to grant us, our day's allowance of Fresh Beef for a Christmas dinner, if it is agreeable to you and the rest of the gentlemen, to whom it may concern." Clarkson was more than happy to comply with Peters's request, noting in his diary that "this pleased them very much."

Unbeknownst to Thomas Peters, it would be more than just his final North American Christmas dinner — it would, in fact, be his very last Christmas celebration.

The fleet of fifteen ships bound for Sierra Leone left Halifax on January 15, 1792. Separated from one another while crossing the Atlantic, the ships arrived in Freetown between the twenty-sixth of February and the ninth of March.

It soon became apparent that Thomas Peters's quest for justice was not at an end with the Black Loyalists' arrival in Freetown. The lots of land promised to the Black Loyalists had not been surveyed. In fact, very little had been done to prepare for their arrival. The land, it turned out, was not to be granted freely but would require the payment of rents. Worse still, the colony was not to be governed by an elected committee of Black Loyalists but by the white agents of the Sierra Leone Company who oversaw the trade in Freetown. On top of all of these disappointments, the African rainy season had just begun and would have deadly consequences for many of the new arrivals.

Thomas Peter's passion for justice would not let him turn a blind eye to the fact that the colony would not be a Black democracy. It wasn't long before he had circulated a petition for the creation of a Black police force and the elimination of the unpopular rents.

Clarkson, who — much to his dismay — had been put in charge of the colony, rejected Peters's petition. The two men who had once been allies in a humanitarian venture had now become political adversaries. Peters wanted the

Black Loyalists to run their own affairs through an elected committee; Clarkson, forced to "accept the government under its present objectionable form," was afraid of the anarchy that might result in straying from the plans of the Sierra Leone Company.

In early April, all of the Black Loyalist settlers gathered to witness a confrontation between Peters and Clarkson. The Englishman feared that Peters was trying to overthrow the colony's government. Peters assured Clarkson that he was simply voicing the concerns of the settlers and was not about to lead a rebellion. Despite Peters's assurances, he and Clarkson would never completely trust one another again.

Things went from bad to worse for Peters. A month later, he was charged with robbery when he was discovered going through the trunk of a settler who had recently died. Peters adamantly denied the charges, swearing that he had only been trying to recover something that was actually his.

After returning the goods and receiving a public reprimand, Peters fell from grace with those he had represented with unwavering dedication for so long. While sufficient time would no doubt have allowed him to regain his credibility and reputation, Peters only had one month left to live. Thomas Peters died on June 25, 1792, at the age of fifty-four. Malaria had stilled the voice that had railed long and loud against injustice in Nova Scotia, New Brunswick and Sierra Leone.

While Thomas Peters could no longer speak out for justice, his legacy would not be forgotten in Sierra Leone. In 2007, Freetown commemorated the bicentennial of slavery's abolishment by renaming one of its older thoroughfares Thomas Peters Street. Five years later, almost 220 years after his death, the people of Sierra Leone's capital city honoured their founder with a statue of Thomas Peters erected outside St. George's Cathedral.

Described by some as the first African American hero and by others as the Black George Washington, Thomas Peters will be remembered in New Brunswick as the man determined to secure equal rights for its Black Loyalist settlers.

CHAPTER 9
Zimri Armstrong: A Man Betrayed

On the surface, Zimri Armstrong's story is much like that of the hundreds of Black Loyalists who settled in New Brunswick. Hearing of the promise of freedom, he escaped from his rebel master and lent his support to the British war effort. Although he fought for the losing side in the American Revolution, Armstrong achieved his goal in joining the British forces — the former slave was now officially recognized as a free man.

The definition of a Black Loyalist began to form as early as 1775 when Lord Dunmore, the last royalist governor of Virginia, granted liberty to "servants, Negroes or others pertaining to Rebels" in the colony who were "able and willing to bear arms." As a result of Dunmore's proclamation, hundreds of enslaved Blacks fled their Patriot masters to join the British.

Four years later, General Clinton, the commander-in-chief of all the British forces stationed in America, expanded on Dunmore's pronouncement by issuing the Philipsburg Proclamation. It promised that "to every Negro who shall desert the Rebel Standard, full Security [would be given] to follow within these Lines, any Occupation which he shall think proper." And with these words, the greatest emancipation of slaves before the American Civil War began.

Although Dunmore's proclamation granted liberty to those who were "able and willing to bear arms," Clinton's decree allowed freed Blacks to choose their service to the Crown. They simply had to "desert." Once inside British lines their "occupations" were theirs to decide. Women cooked, sewed, set up tents, delivered messages, nursed, cleaned clothes and waited on tables. Black men, though they were not allowed to bear arms, became river pilots and guides for the British army and spies for the British commanders. Some were drummers and trumpeters; others worked as wagon drivers and sailors. In the end, following the Philipsburg Proclamation, thousands of Blacks, including women and children, crossed British lines and became free citizens of the British Empire.

For Zimri Armstrong, this meant that he was now free to board any of the evacuation vessels that were carrying soldiers and Loyalist refugees to sanctuary outside the United States of America. But taking advantage of free passage to Nova Scotia, Canada, Britain, the West Indies or the German states was not Armstrong's first concern. Although the British had made him free, the Black Loyalist's wife and children were still slaves. And time was running out.

With the British occupation of New York City entering its final weeks, there was simply no time to earn the money he needed to purchase his family's release. Returning to his former master's home to liberate them was impossible. Seeing no other solution, Armstrong made a desperate gamble.

The Black Loyalist's only assets were his time and labour, but they could be worth a great deal to the right employer. By becoming an indentured servant, Armstrong reasoned, he could use his time and labour to free his wife and children from slavery. The Black Loyalist decided to offer two years of service to any white Loyalist who would agree to purchase Armstrong's family and set them free.

It was a solution that required patience. The Armstrong family would not be reunited until 1785 at the earliest, but the 1783 indenture agreement promised long-term benefits that would more than compensate for the family's temporary separation.

Indentures were commonplace throughout the eighteenth century, so when Zimri Armstrong finally sat down with Samuel Jarvis to work out the details of their agreement, both men knew what was expected of them. A Loyalist from Connecticut, Jarvis was very familiar with legal documents. He had spent the final years of the revolution handling public accounts and papers in the British commissary general's department in New York City.

Despite the defeat of the royal army, the future looked bright for the Jarvis family. Having proved himself a trusted civil servant in New York, Samuel was invited to remain in the employ of the commissary general when its staff returned to Britain. An indentured servant such as Zimri Armstrong would prove very useful as the Jarvises adapted to life in the motherland.

Armstrong had a good record of service as well. During the revolution, the Black Loyalist had been a member of a company of Loyalist soldiers under the command of John Wetmore. And there was no question as to Armstrong's status as a free man. Only free men and women could enter into indenture agreements.

Although the period for indentures was typically seven to ten years, Armstrong and Jarvis worked out the details for a two-year arrangement. In addition to the standard provision of food and clothing, Jarvis agreed to purchase and liberate Armstrong's family, set the Black Loyalist up in a trade and cover the cost of any travel expenses. Armstrong, for his part, would serve the Jarvis family for twenty-four months, going wherever they went and fulfilling whatever tasks were asked of him.

While the terms of the indenture were not unusual, the times in which they were negotiated certainly were. The British had promised to give their Black allies grants of land in Nova Scotia as well as the basic provisions that they would require during their first year of settlement. However, these benefits did not extend to the enslaved Blacks owned by white Loyalists or to any indentured Black Loyalists.

By becoming an indentured servant, Zimri Armstrong was forfeiting the opportunity to have his own land in the northern colonies. No doubt this is why his indenture included the clause that Jarvis would set him up in a trade; a marketable skill would compensate for the land that he lost as an indentured servant.

Zimri Armstrong's plan would have worked if he had found the right Loyalist. However, Samuel Jarvis was not a man to be trusted. It was only after the two men had settled in New Brunswick that Armstrong would realize the depths of Jarvis's betrayal.

The Jarvis family's time in Great Britain came to an abrupt end. Just months after his arrival from New York City, Samuel was informed that the British army no longer required his services. With no other sources of income, Jarvis needed to move quickly to resolve his family's crisis.

Financial uncertainty for his employer endangered Zimri Armstrong's future as well. His indenture was an asset that the Jarvis family could sell to someone else — someone who, living in Great Britain, would have little concern for Armstrong's family enslaved across the ocean in America. Returning to Connecticut was not an option for the Jarvis family, given the hatred the victorious Americans had for Loyalists and it certainly was not an option for Armstrong, who would be immediately re-enslaved.

Parrtown, however, was an option. By August of 1784, the territory had been made into its own colony and was in need of farmers, entrepreneurs, merchants and civil servants. And, as it turned out, several of Jarvis's siblings were already living in the colony. Loyalists from Connecticut had settled in such great numbers along the nearby Kennebecasis River that it was referred to as the "Yankee Shore." Samuel's older brother, Munson Jarvis, was in the process of establishing a mercantile company in Parrtown; New Brunswick seemed like an ideal fit.

With Zimri Armstrong in tow, Jarvis and his family crossed the Atlantic once again and settled among the Loyalists of Parrtown where Samuel managed to secure a position as a government surveyor. Armstrong soon discovered that he also had his own contacts within New Brunswick.

The men the Black Loyalist had served with during the American Revolution had settled in the colony, including their senior officer, Captain John Wetmore. They were in the midst of clearing the land they had been granted, drawing on provisions freely supplied by the local British garrison until they could grow their own food.

However, New Brunswick proved to be yet another disappointment for Samuel Jarvis. Conditions in Parrtown were primitive compared to those they had enjoyed in New York and England and a major summer fire had devastated the city, reducing most of the settlement's log cabins to charred ruins. Although Jarvis's brother John lived upriver in Kingston, he had become an alcoholic and was completely incapable of caring for his family or providing them with adequate shelter. Their sister Polly had become a widow when her husband died by his own hand and the Parrtown fire had levelled her home, making her totally reliant on her three brothers for support. Added to all of this was the fact that Samuel's wife was expecting their third child in the spring of 1785.

Connecticut, an unthinkable option just a year earlier, was too tantalizing to ignore. Besides his widowed mother, Samuel's Patriot siblings still had homes in Stamford and rebel anger against Loyalists was beginning to subside. Turning his back on the paltry rewards of loyalty to the Crown, Jarvis sold his Parrtown grant, gathered up his family and sailed for Connecticut. But unlike their earlier journeys to England and New Brunswick, the Jarvises did not bring Zimri Armstrong with them.

Safeguarding one the few assets left to him, Jarvis transferred the Black Loyalist's indenture over to his brother, John Jarvis. Although the two-year agreement was nearing its end, Armstrong was obligated to honour his indenture contract until the following summer. Of course,

Samuel Jarvis had his obligations as well. The Black Loyalist assumed that after his employer returned to Connecticut, the latter would fulfill the terms of Armstrong's indenture by securing the freedom of his family.

Armstrong continued to honour his contractual obligations, working through the fall and winter. But with summer's arrival, it was clear that something was wrong. Samuel Jarvis had sent no word of having purchased Armstrong's family and John Jarvis had not given the Black Loyalist the clothes or provisions promised to him in the indenture. Furthermore, he had received no training in a trade. A free man once more, Zimri Armstrong was completely destitute. But he had not lost his determination.

Armstrong sought out Munson Jarvis in Saint John and demanded that the merchant's family honour its contract with him. Samuel's brother refused to have anything to do with the Black Loyalist. Armstrong was left "destitute of both clothes and provisions in a strange country," and neither of the Jarvis brothers in New Brunswick had, in Armstrong's own words, given him "the value of one penny to support me when I was not able to support myself."

But the Jarvis betrayal went far beyond reneging on clothes, food and money. To his horror, Armstrong heard rumours that when Samuel Jarvis returned to Connecticut, he had, as agreed, sought out the Black Loyalists' family — but not with the intent of purchasing their freedom. According to the rumours, Jarvis had, in Armstrong's words, "gone back and sold my wife and family."

Fearful that this might be the truth, Armstrong tried to discover what had transpired in Connecticut. He sought out George Leonard, a Massachusetts Loyalist who had been appointed as an agent of the British government in

Parrtown. The Black Loyalist requested that Leonard summon John Jarvis to appear before the agent and be made to fulfill his half of the indenture agreement. Leonard did as he was asked. Upon John Jarvis's arrival in Parrtown, he took an oath saying that his brother Samuel would be returning to New Brunswick within six weeks to carry out the terms of the Black Loyalist's indenture.

For a brief moment, it seemed that Zimri Armstrong would receive the justice due him. However, at the end of six weeks, there was no Samuel Jarvis to be seen. Instead, Armstrong received confirmation from a credible source that Jarvis had, indeed, sold his wife and children.

Once again, the Black Loyalist appealed to George Leonard and once again the British agent called on John Jarvis. On this occasion, John admitted that his brother Samuel had sold Armstrong's wife and children. Despite his brother's shameful betrayal, John would not honour any of the other obligations set out in Armstrong's indenture agreement.

When pressed to provide Armstrong with the promised provisions, John Jarvis sought out John Wetmore, the captain of Armstrong's company and tried to convince him to give the Black Loyalist some of the basic supplies that had been distributed to the members of Wetmore's corps. Wetmore would only agree to this scheme if he received an order from a recognized authority.

Zimri's next step was to appeal to Thomas Knox, the deputy commissioner of musters. Once a member of the British staff in New York City during the American Revolution, Knox was now in charge of dispensing provisions to New Brunswick's Loyalist refugees. He had learned of John Jarvis's refusal to provide for Armstrong as well as Jarvis's failed attempt to siphon off provisions from the Black Loyalist's disbanded company. Knox came to Armstrong's aid by giving him official authorization to receive flour and meat.

The Black Loyalist's immediate needs were satisfied; but the larger justice issues still had to be addressed. Having received all the assistance that the officials in Parrtown and Fort Howe could give him, Armstrong decided to direct an appeal to Lieutenant-Governor Carleton.

When he had found someone to serve as his scribe, Armstrong dictated a petition to Carleton that laid out the story of Samuel Jarvis's disregard for his indenture agreement. While other Black Loyalists wrote memorials asking for land grants, Armstrong's was the only petition addressed to the lieutenant-governor to register a complaint against a white Loyalist. It is a unique example of how a Black Loyalist sought justice for himself.

Armstrong knew the value of documents and personal references. In an effort to win Thomas Carleton to his cause, he offered to "produce the paper about our agreement between me and Samuel Jarvis." He also had "credible people in this town" who would vouch for all that he had written in his petition.

Zimri Armstrong did not ask the New Brunswick government to train him in a trade or purchase his family for him. Despite the fact that Jarvis had left him "destitute of both clothes and provisions in a Strange Country," Armstrong knew that he could not expect Carleton to fulfill all of the terms of his indenture. Instead, the Black Loyalist asked that he be given what he had forfeited in becoming an indentured servant. His request was that "if there is any land to spare, to grant me some." He finished his memorial with the hope that he would be treated in the same manner as other "indigent loyalists."

It is important to note that Armstrong saw no distinction between himself and New Brunswick's white Loyalists. His time as a slave and then as an indentured servant had not diminished his innate sense of self worth. Now a citizen of the British Empire, he expected to be treated as an equal to his fellow colonists.

Despite documentation, character references and the support of other Loyalists, Zimri Armstrong's hopes that he would receive justice were shattered. After considering the Black Loyalist's petition on June 21, 1785, the lieutenant-governor said that there was nothing he could do to help Armstrong. While the courts were another means by which he could seek restitution, a penniless and illiterate man in Armstrong's circumstances could proceed no further.

Two years of indentured service had failed to earn Zimri Armstrong his family, provisions, clothes or a trade and because of his temporary servant status, he was not able to receive the land that was granted to other Black Loyalists — all because of Samuel Jarvis's breach of faith.

Armstrong spent the next six years as one of the scores of unskilled labourers within New Brunswick's Black Loyalist community, but his fortunes took a sudden turn for the better in the fall of 1791 when a Black war veteran returned from a visit to Great Britain with promises of a fresh start for Black Loyalists in Sierra Leone.

Among those who jumped at this chance for a fresh start was Zimri Armstrong.

The agent appointed to oversee the departure of the colony's Black Loyalists did all he could to obstruct their exodus from New Brunswick. Faced with the prospect of losing a source of inexpensive labour, the agent fabricated reasons to detain worthy Black Loyalists. He demanded to see their 1783 Birch certificates, warned that Black Loyalists would be sold as slaves when they reached Sierra Leone and accepted as legitimate the indenture contracts that had been forged to prevent Blacks from leaving New Brunswick. Others refused to pay Black Loyalists their wages, thinking that a lack of money would prevent them from leaving the colony.

Despite all of these obstructions, 222 Black Loyalists, including Zimri Armstrong, successfully boarded ships bound for Halifax that December. After vessels with passengers from Nova Scotia's Black Loyalist settlements joined those from New Brunswick, the combined fleet left Halifax for Sierra Leone on January 15, 1792.

Like Thomas Peters, Zimri Armstrong found the new promised land was not everything he had been led to expect. This was not the free Black democracy they had been promised and in the years that followed, deadly diseases, religious squabbles, outside attacks and civil unrest bedeviled the Black settlers of Freetown. Frustrated with how the Sierra Leone Company continually thwarted their efforts to own land and govern themselves, 150 men gathered in one of Freetown's chapels on September 10, 1800, to consider their options. By the end of the evening, those assembled had agreed upon a complete break from the Sierra Leone Company. It was the beginning of what came to be called the Nova Scotian Rebellion.

Three leaders emerged from the meeting in the chapel; men who were recognized as the strongest opponents to company rule and who were the most articulate when it came to voicing Black Loyalists' frustration. John Cuthbert, who had been a Baptist elder in Birchtown, Nova Scotia, was made the rebellion's judicial officer. Isaac Anderson, a Black Loyalist born free in Charleston, South Carolina, was the consensus leader. And Zimri Armstrong, who had settled in Saint John, New Brunswick, was appointed the secretary. Doubtless, Armstrong's experience with the broken promises of white men helped to fuel his animosity towards the authorities in Freetown.

Events unfolded slowly. The rebels announced their new constitution for Sierra Leone on the tenth of September and then presented it to the people of Freetown on the twenty-fifth. The following day, the Sierra Leone Company's governor sent an armed guard to arrest the men who had signed the rebel's constitution but it was only able to capture one man.

The rebels declared Isaac Anderson their new governor on the twenty-seventh, underscoring this fact by capturing a bridge just outside of Freetown. A force of fifty rebels then stood watch for the next four days, nervously waiting for the Sierra Leone Company's men to launch an attack. On the second of October, a force of 150 stormed the rebel position, killing two and capturing thirty men.

Where Zimri Armstrong was during this battle is uncertain. Records do not reveal whether he was one of its casualties or one of the thirty-four rebels who appeared before a military court a week later. Isaac Anderson and one of his fellow rebels were found guilty of treason and executed. Thirty-two others were banished.

With no record of Zimri Armstrong's fate, it is likely that he was banished, rather than hanged, for his role in the revolt. Seven of the Black Loyalists who escaped the gallows were sent to Senegal's Goree Island and twenty-five were exiled to the Bullom Shore along Sierra Leone's northern coast. Within a matter of weeks, those who had spearheaded the short-lived Nova Scotian Rebellion had been executed, exiled or discredited.

The Black Loyalists who made their homes in New Brunswick confronted betrayal and injustice on a daily basis, but few bore the destructive intensity of a racist society to the same degree as Zimri Armstrong. During the American Revolution, he escaped from his rebel master on the gamble that life as a free man would be better than that of a slave.

For the duration of the war, Armstrong risked life and limb as he supported the British, only to face the prospect of re-enslavement at the end of the war. After suffering the loss of his family and fortune through the duplicity of a white Loyalist, he was denied justice by the New Brunswick government. When he prepared to leave the colony six years later, corrupt officials fabricated bureaucratic obstacles in an attempt to prevent his departure.

Upon his arrival in Sierra Leone, Armstrong's efforts to achieve equality and prosperity were once again thwarted by institutionalized racism. Neither the Sierra Leone trading company nor the British authorities considered free Blacks capable of governing themselves.

Finally, after eight years of being denied their rights as free citizens of the British Empire, Armstrong and his fellow Black Loyalists resorted to rebellion. In the end, their aspirations to create a fair and equitable society were crushed. The dream of liberty, ignited during the American Revolution, had been extinguished by a series of nightmares, ending in banishment.

Zimri Armstrong was, by all accounts, a man most thoroughly betrayed.

CHAPTER 10
Richard Corankapoon: A Determined Leader

When Lieutenant John Clarkson opened the door of his Halifax lodgings late on December 9, 1791, he was startled to find four Africans standing in the cold and dark. Since the English abolitionist was in charge of organizing a fleet of ships to take Black Loyalists to Sierra Leone, he was accustomed to receiving needy visitors — but none with the story this quartet had to tell.

Six months earlier, the British government had responded to the injustices experienced by Black Loyalists in Nova Scotia and New Brunswick by offering them the opportunity to have their own colony in West Africa. Expecting that only a few hundred would respond to the offer, Clarkson was overwhelmed when almost twelve thousand Black Loyalists signed up for the chance to become Sierra Leone's founders. Over the past weeks, these Black Loyalists had travelled to

Halifax by sailing vessels and prepared themselves to board the fifteen ships bound for Africa. The reason these four men walked to Halifax to come to Clarkson's door was beyond the Englishman's imagination.

Once inside Clarkson's house, the travellers shared their story. The four Black Loyalists had spent the last two weeks travelling on foot to Halifax from Saint John, New Brunswick — a distance of almost five hundred kilometres. Clarkson's shock and surprise are evident in his diary as he recounted the gist of the four men's story.

> *These people were determined to quit a country, at the peril of their lives, whose inhabitants treated them with so much barbarity; they had the temerity to undertake a journey over land from St. John to Halifax...they set out for this Purpose the 24th last month, went round the head of the Bay of Fundy, & notwithstanding they had to combat with difficulties, that might appear insuperable to a considerate mind principally arising from the extreme closeness of woods and the river they would be under the necessity of fording, they arrived safe & in good health, fifteen days after their departure from St. Johns.*
>
> *The greatest distress must have driven these men to form a resolution so uncommon and to preserve a journey so replete with danger & difficulty, their passage for a few days being through such parts as I am convinced were never before visited by man.*

One of the four Black Loyalists who undertook this amazing overland journey had once been known as Richard Wheeler. Going to extremes to achieve his goals was a hallmark of this most remarkable man.

Slave traders had captured Wheeler as a youth in his West African homeland. Forced to endure the middle passage across the Atlantic, he arrived in America where he was sold as a slave. In time, he became the property of Caleb Wheeler of New Jersey and was given the name Richard. Fortunately for him, Richard was among those enslaved Africans who were permitted to learn a trade in the New World. His newly acquired skills allowed him to earn his own money despite being a slave. Rather than spending his earnings on immediate needs, Richard put his money aside, saving until he was able to purchase his freedom from his master. In 1776, at the age of twenty-three, Richard embarked on his new life as a free man.

It was not the safest of times to be an emancipated Black man. The American Revolution had begun just the year before. Had he fallen into rebel hands, Richard Wheeler could easily have had his hard won freedom invalidated and been made a slave once again. Although American Patriots claimed to fight for "liberty," they had absolutely no desire to set their Black slaves free. The best option for Wheeler was to support the war efforts of the only white men who promised to recognize his status as a free man — the commanders of the British forces based in New York City. Though Wheeler and many others made their way to New York City, any city occupied by the British during the revolution, such as Savannah, Georgia, Charleston, South Carolina, or Philadelphia, Pennsylvania, were also places of refuge for displaced persons loyal to the Crown.

After seven years of service to King George III, Wheeler received a Birch certificate to affirm his status as a free Black Loyalist. But this was not all that Wheeler received from the British authorities. He was also given a title and a job.

Thousands of civilians had been streaming into New York City to escape persecution at the hands of the victorious American Patriots. To better facilitate their transportation and settlement, Sir Guy Carleton, the British commander-in-chief, organized the Loyalists into companies under the command of an appointed captain. Rather than a military rank, this title gave official recognition to key civilians in the unprecedented task of evacuating thousands of refugees. As part of their responsibilities, refugee company captains served as intermediaries between local authorities and the people they led. They would receive directives from Carleton or the captains of their evacuation vessels and be sources of information for the evacuees in their care. They were also responsible for ensuring that their company members boarded their evacuation ship on the appropriate date.

On the last day of July 1783, four companies of Black Loyalists boarded the *Clinton*, a ship bound for Annapolis Royal and the mouth of the St. John River. In recognition of his capabilities as a leader, the British authorities appointed Richard Wheeler as the captain of one of the four companies. His group comprised thirty-four husbands and bachelors who set sail along with the *Clinton*'s other 242 Black passengers.

Wheeler's company was a diverse one, made up of people ranging in age from sixteen to forty-five. Originally enslaved in New Jersey, Wheeler was now the leader of men who had escaped slavery in Virginia, Pennsylvania and New York as well as New Jersey.

The Black evacuees that Wheeler met before the *Clinton*

left New York City not only shared his two-week journey north, but would establish their first homes in the same refugee settlement as Wheeler. They would become the nucleus of a new community of free Black men and women in New Brunswick.

The Black Loyalists who did not have Wheeler as their company's captain came to know him as a neighbour after they received their town lots in Carleton. In the months that followed, a part of their regular routine would be to cross the harbour and walk up the steep hill to Fort Howe to receive their rations — potatoes, flour, butter, peas, oatmeal, beef and pork — from the commissary.

Less than a year after his arrival in New Brunswick, Wheeler had become so confident in his new status as a free man that he began to make efforts to reclaim his African name. The first evidence for this is found in Fort Howe's victualling muster for June 1784 where, with the addition of a seemingly insignificant single initial, the young man's name was recorded as Richard C. Wheeler. Within a year, a petition bearing Wheeler's name would reveal the meaning of that initial.

In January of 1785, as the captain of one of the Black Loyalist companies that had settled in Carleton, Richard Wheeler's name was the first of fifteen names to be listed on a petition to New Brunswick's lieutenant-governor. The petition asked Thomas Carleton for either land or "relief in their wretched circumstances" for its Black signatories. In standing up for the rights of those he lead, Wheeler felt it was important to write out his full name, which now included his African name as well as the name he had been given as a slave.

It was not an easy name for English speakers to pronounce or spell. There are no less than six different spellings for

Wheeler's African name in the era's documents: Crankapone, Corankeapoon, Corankapoon, Corankapone, Corankapon and Crankipine. As "Corankapoon" is the spelling given on the lands grant that Wheeler and his company eventually received, this is the spelling that will be used in this account. Sometime after 1787, Wheeler dropped his New Jersey enslaver's surname entirely and became known simply as Richard Corankapoon.

Besides Corankapoon, only five other Black Loyalists who settled in New Brunswick are known to have retained their African names: Cuff Fairchild, a fifty-five-year-old runaway from Connecticut; Cuff Potter, a fifty-three-year-old Birch certificate holder from Rhode Island; Cuff Ben, who escaped enslavement in Virginia; and Cuffie, a forty-year-old man from New York. Their common first name is the English rendering of "Kofi," a name found among the Akan people of Ghana.

The fifth New Brunswick Black Loyalist who is known to have kept his African name is Johmall Cole. His name appears in the probate record of another free Black man. In writing down "Johmall," the court official was obviously trying to spell "Jamal," a Muslim name that would have been found in parts of West Africa. Since the time of his capture by slave traders, Cole had been able to retain the name his African parents had given him — an Arabic word meaning "handsome." The fact that he was able to keep his own name despite decades of enslavement demonstrates that Cole had as strong a character and innate sense of worth as Richard Corankapoon.

Eight of the fifteen names on Corankapoon's 1785 petition to Thomas Carleton were men who had sailed with him on the *Clinton*. They appealed to the New Brunswick government for land so they could "lead industrious, honest lives" and be "an advantage to the community." The small town lots they had initially received across the harbour from Parrtown were not sufficient to provide them with the necessary food and shelter. The petitioners were "under apprehensions of suffering this winter, labour and provisions being so very scarce."

Corankapoon reminded the colonial government that "the Blacks in general have been thought loyal and have throughout the rebellion been generally ready to obey any orders." He affirmed that "the same disposition will remain among them" once they were settled on reasonable land grants.

Lieutenant-Governor Thomas Carleton did not hold the same regard for his colony's free Blacks as his brother Sir Guy Carleton had demonstrated during the days of the Loyalist evacuation of New York. Where Guy boldly risked violating the peace treaty that ended the American Revolution in order to secure the emancipation of the loyal Blacks, Thomas saw them as a nuisance.

In a letter to the British secretary of state, Thomas Carleton wrote, "Among the free Negroes settled in this province, I have found only three who appear to have been ever employed in any military service. These have had their allotments with their respective corps. The rest are such as . . . are denominated Black Refugees, who having come within the British lines to escape the service of their American masters cannot be considered as entitled to claim anything from Government further than personal protection and freedom from servitude, which they enjoy in consequence of arrangements made by the Commander in Chief previous to the evacuation of New York for granting them an asylum in this country."

Carleton felt that sufficient charity had been extended to men such as Corankapoon when they arrived in the colony in 1783 and "lots were granted the Black Refugees at St. John where many of them remained until the provisions granted by the government were exhausted."

Carleton felt that these measures were sufficient, noting that the Blacks had "been allowed every privilege of free British subjects, nor has any distinction been made between them and the white inhabitants, excepting only that they have not been admitted to vote in Elections for representatives in the General Assembly."

Where Corankapoon regarded his people as full British citizens, the white Loyalists of New Brunswick considered them to be free — but not equal — before the law. Nevertheless, the colonial government eventually made a positive response to the Black Loyalists' petition for land.

On July 25, 1786, New Brunswick granted Corankapoon and his fifteen Black Loyalist associates land along the Nerepis River, a tributary of the St. John River not far from present day Westfield. How the Black settlers survived on their insufficient town lots in the intervening year and a half goes unrecorded. Corankapoon's patience and determination had given the impoverished Black Loyalists of Saint John a second chance at prosperity.

In 1787, four years after their arrival in New Brunswick, Corankapoon and his compatriots were finally given official title to grants along the Nerepis River. Written in the formal legal language of the day and bearing the great seal of New Brunswick, the document must have been seen as confirmation that the Black Loyalists' fortunes had finally changed for the better.

Although their Nerepis land grants had been given with the best of intentions, Corankapoon and his associates did not fare any better there than they had on their town lots in Saint John. As one historian of the early twentieth century phrased it, it was hoped that the Black Loyalists would "acquire habits of industry and forethought, without which freedom could be to them no real benefit." Despite the desire of one of Corankapoon's neighbours to "raise as much grain and vegetables as lays in my power," no amount of work or planning could overcome the obstacles to success encountered by the Black Loyalist settlers.

The Nerepis grants were not outright gifts, but instead were leases that required an annual payment of one shilling for every fifty acres. The Black Loyalists' lots were not large enough or clear enough to grow sufficient food for their families. Despite Corankapoon's determination and his neighbours' best intentions, the Black Loyalists could not realistically pursue a living from the land. In the end, most of the sixteen families moved to towns and villages where they hired out their labour to white Loyalists.

Frustrated at every turn, the Black Loyalists who had initially settled in Saint John and then the nearby river valleys were, four years after their arrival, still dependent on the meager wages that white Loyalists paid them for strenuous physical labour. Other Blacks had no option but to become indentured servants, bartering away years of their lives in exchange for shelter and food. The issues of insufficient land grants and the denial of the basic rights of British citizenship needed a champion.

That champion was Thomas Peters, the Black Pioneers sergeant who travelled to England in 1791 to seek justice for Blacks from the British government and came back with news of a free Black colony in Sierra Leone. Having been frustrated in establishing a community for those who had accompanied him to New Brunswick in 1783, Corankapoon decided to join with other Black Loyalists who saw Sierra Leone as the best hope for the realization of their dreams. But the New Brunswick agent appointed to oversee the process of settler applications for Sierra Leone did everything in his power to deny these applications and almost succeeded in keeping Corankapoon in New Brunswick. Among those denied passage on board the ships bound for Halifax from Saint John in November of 1791 were four men who would not take no for an answer. Their leader, not surprisingly, was Richard Corankapoon.

And so it was that after a fifteen day trek through the forests of New Brunswick and Nova Scotia, Corankapoon and his companions made their way to the door of Lieutenant John Clarkson, the man in charge of overseeing the Black Loyalists' journey to Sierra Leone. Clarkson marvelled at the barbarity of New Brunswick's authorities that had forced the men "at the peril of their lives" to "form a resolution so uncommon" that they gambled their lives to journey overland to Halifax.

When 1,196 Black Loyalists finally sailed out of Halifax for Sierra Leone on January 15, 1792, they held certificates that entitled the bearers to free grants of land in the new colony. Within seven weeks, the fleet of fifteen ships finally dropped anchor near a peninsula just off the mouth of Tagrin Bay, Sierra Leone. This became the site of Freetown, the capital of the new colony.

However, the land that the Black Loyalists expected to receive was slow in being distributed. The promised fortifications had not been built and the land had not been cleared or surveyed. Still in need of a governor for the colony, the Sierra Leone Company appointed Corankapoon's new friend, Lieutenant John Clarkson, to oversee the new settlement. The twenty-eight-year-old bachelor had been looking forward to immediately returning to England, but he felt responsible for the Black Loyalists and remained in Freetown.

The lack of proper preparation was nothing new to the Black Loyalists; it had been the same when they arrived on the shores of Nova Scotia and New Brunswick in 1783. But the fledgling Loyalist African community had a valuable asset in men such as Corankapoon, who had many experiences with petitioning local governments.

By December, Corankapoon's name was on a petition to the directors of the Sierra Leone Company, asking on behalf of a majority of settlers that they allow Lieutenant Clarkson to continue as the colony's governor. But it was not to be. The young lieutenant was recalled to England, never to see his Black Loyalist friends again.

But Corankapoon and Clarkson did not forget each other. Corankapoon kept in touch with Clarkson, confiding in a letter that "the Body of the Colleny is Bent for your honer to Com and Be our governor." For his part, Clarkson made a point of trying to fulfil the Black Loyalist's request to track down the British army officers who had assisted Corankapoon during his service in the revolution. Records of the era fail to say whether the Black Loyalist ever made contact with his former commanding officer.

As had happened in New York and then in New Brunswick, those in authority in Sierra Leone quickly recognized Corankapoon's leadership qualities and he served as both a marshal and a constable for the next two governors.

Just over a year after the Black Loyalists arrived in Freetown, an incident almost led to an insurrection. A slave trader named Grierson insulted two Nova Scotians (as the Black Loyalists now called themselves) and when the men of Freetown retaliated by harassing the slave trader, the colonial governor intervened. But rather than charging Grierson, the governor settled the matter by dismissing the two men the slave trader had insulted.

On Friday, June 20, 1794, the Black settlers demanded an explanation for the dismissals. Richard Corankapoon tried to break up the mob, but was attacked by two fellow New Brunswick settlers who went so far as to threaten to hang him. A warrant was promptly issued for the arrest of the two attackers and in short order, riots broke out, lasting three days. In the end, eight ringleaders were sent to England for trial and the other rebels were banished from the colony.

Although this riot was contained, dissatisfaction with the Sierra Leone Company continued to fester in the years that followed. By October 1800, the situation boiled over into outright rebellion. It must have been a difficult situation for Corankapoon. Three of the rebel leaders were men he had known since the days they had settled together in New Brunswick twenty years earlier.

Corankapoon and another marshal went to arrest the rebel leaders, resulting in claims that the two officers had used excessive force. Some witnesses said that the marshals found unarmed rebels in a house and immediately began to fire on them, forcing the leaders to defend themselves with fence rails. Corankapoon asserted that the rebels attacked them with clubs, knocking out the other marshal, which compelled him to fire upon their assailants. Because of his position with the Sierra Leone Company, some of those in Freetown were beginning to see Corankapoon as a tool of the white government.

The growing fervor for self-government began to escalate the situation, which eventually culminated in a battle between the rebels and those loyal to the governor. As he had in 1776, Corankapoon sided with the governing authority of the day. In the end, the Sierra Leone Company "loyalists" overwhelmed the rebels thanks to the timely appearance of the *Asia*, a supply ship from England that had just arrived in Freetown. Its crew was instrumental in quickly quashing the rebellion. Thirty-three rebels were banished and two were hanged.

Among those who were banished was Nathaniel Wansey. Seventeen years earlier, Wansey had been a member of Richard Corankapoon's company aboard the *Clinton* and had settled alongside his captain in Carleton, New Brunswick. Later, he was one of the unsuccessful farmers who, along with Corankapoon, had tried to establish a farm on the shores of the Nerepis River. As the American Revolution had done two decades earlier, the Sierra Leone rebellion tore long established friends apart, never to be restored.

A year after his banishment, Wansey and a war party of local Africans attacked Freetown. Richard Corankapoon once again put himself between armed attackers and the recognized government, but this time he paid with his life. After surviving the violence of slavery and the American Revolution and the tribulations of settling in New Brunswick's wilderness, Richard Corankapoon died at the age of forty-eight defending his new Sierra Leone homeland.

Less than a decade after the arrival of the Black Loyalists in the West African colony, one of its most capable leaders was dead. Richard Corankapoon's life ended as it had been lived — with determination and dedication. Had his talents been given their due regard in New Brunswick, the Black Loyalist could have been a dynamic community leader. He knew how to make use of the political system to achieve justice for his people. Even in a racist society, he commanded the trust of whites in positions of authority. Faced with the prospect of having to walk almost five hundred kilometres overland in the winter, his determination did not waiver. When he put his mind to a task, he achieved his goals.

Richard Corankapoon's accomplishments demonstrate the potential contributions that Black Loyalists could have made to New Brunswick society — a potential thwarted by a racist mindset that was not able to see beyond the colour of a man's skin.

CONCLUSION

An Advantage to the Community

If the experiences shared during the tumult of war or in the midst of cataclysmic events have the power to bind people together, then New Brunswick's white and Black Loyalist settlers had experienced more than enough to give them common ground. Both groups had suffered violence at the hands of Patriots during the American Revolution and both had faced the prospect of having their concerns sacrificed in the interest of reaching a speedy peace at war's end. Each group braved a two-week sea journey to find sanctuary in the northern wilderness and each had to create homes in virgin forests with nothing but the labour of their hands.

Both groups of Loyalists suffered through a first winter in New Brunswick that began early and lasted a long time. They each had to make do with the provisions provided by a garrison's commissary, never losing the hope that they could eke a living out of the land once spring arrived. But where Black Loyalists were ready to embrace the rights and responsibilities of British citizenship, the white Loyalists could not conceive of any social order that did not have Blacks on its bottom-most rung.

An early Loyalist settler had proudly declared, "we will be the envy of the American states . . . when the people of the neighbouring states shall observe our operations . . . and compare their state with ours, will they not envy us? Surely they will." It was a hollow dream for the Black Loyalists.

As the stories of the nine lives in this book have shown, there was very little to envy in their New Brunswick experience. Thomas Hide, Richard Corankapoon, Thomas Peters and Edward Burr were all frustrated in their twin attempts to secure good farm land and establish Black communities. While Nancy Mosley was fortunate enough to be treated as an equal before the courts, the concerns of Black Loyalists were usually dismissed as being inconsequential, as they were in the case of Zimri Armstrong's broken indenture agreement. Edward Burr and a handful of other Black Loyalists had been able to amass some worldly goods, but ten times their number, feeling that they had nothing to lose, bet their lives on the possibility of prosperity in Sierra Leone. Even in death, the Black Loyalists were segregated from their white neighbours and were denied burial in common graveyards.

And yet, despite the difficult and often tragic course of their lives, the Black Loyalists of New Brunswick persevered. Thomas Peters made a transatlantic journey to seek justice for his people. Richard Corankapoon walked almost 500 kilometres through snow laden woods to board a ship for Sierra Leone. Pompey Rumsey gave up the privileges of being a free man to be near his enslaved wife. Edward Burr used music to rise above the lowly status of gravedigger. John Patterson and Zimri Armstrong gambled that they could eventually enjoy life as free men by temporarily becoming indentured servants. Thomas Hide weathered the loss of his white employer and used his new found rights as a British citizen to petition a white government for land — something he would never have imagined doing back in Connecticut. They were all people who, in their own way, refused to be treated as anything less than free men and women.

Had they been allowed to do so, Black Loyalists would have made greater contributions during the early days of New Brunswick's settlement. Time and again their petitions to the colonial government spoke of their desire to "lead industrious, honest lives" so that they could be "an advantage to the community." The limitations that the Black Loyalists faced were imposed upon them by a racist society, thwarting their attempts at advancement at every turn.

Despite all of this, the historical documents of the day — few as they are — show that the Black Loyalists of New Brunswick maintained an indomitable spirit. Today that heritage of perseverance is being remembered and celebrated as never before as communities along the St. John River are beginning to acknowledge their early Black founders. Since 2009, the King's Landing Historical Settlement has featured a Black settler's house.

Several geographical features in New Brunswick underwent name changes in the early twenty-first century in recognition of the province's Black Loyalist heritage. Negro Lake near Grand Bay-Westfield is now Corankapone Lake in honour of Richard Wheeler. What was once known as Negro Brook in the same community has become Black

Loyalist Brook. Negro Point near Saint John was renamed Hodges Point to honour a Black Loyalist family.

Two hundred years is a long time to wait, but the contributions of New Brunswick's neglected founders are slowly being recognized and celebrated. Their names are no longer forgotten. The stories of the Black Loyalists of New Brunswick shared here are a contribution to this remembering and a testimony to a people who, having seized the opportunity to be free, persevered despite overwhelming odds.

Index